THE ALEXANDER SHAKESPEARE

General Editor
R.B. Kennedy

Additional notes and editing
Mike Gould

RICHARD II

William Shakespeare

COLLINS
CLASSICS

Harper Press
An imprint of HarperCollins*Publishers*
77–85 Fulham Palace Road
Hammersmith
London W6 8JB

This Harper Press paperback edition published 2011

A catalogue record for this book is available from the British Library

ISBN-13: 978-0-00-790229-3

Printed and bound in Great Britain by Clays Ltd, St Ives plc

MIX
Paper from
responsible sources
FSC™ C007454

www.fsc.org

FSC™ is a non-profit international organisation established to promote
the responsible management of the world's forests. Products carrying the
FSC label are independently certified to assure consumers that they come
from forests that are managed to meet the social, economic and
ecological needs of present and future generations,
and other controlled sources.

Find out more about HarperCollins and the environment at
www.harpercollins.co.uk/green

Life & Times section © Gerard Cheshire
Introduction by Robert Grant
Shakespeare: Words and Phrases adapted from
Collins English Dictionary
Typesetting in Kalix by Palimpsest Book Production Limited,
Falkirk, Stirlingshire

10 9 8 7 6 5 4 3 2 1

Prefatory Note

This Shakespeare play uses the full Alexander text. By keeping in mind the fact that the language has changed considerably in four hundred years, as have customs, jokes, and stage conventions, the editors have aimed at helping the modern reader – whether English is their mother tongue or not – to grasp the full significance of the play. The Notes, intended primarily for examination candidates, are presented in a simple, direct style. The needs of those unfamiliar with British culture have been specially considered.

Since quiet study of the printed word is unlikely to bring fully to life plays that were written directly for the public theatre, attention has been drawn to dramatic effects which are important in performance. The editors see Shakespeare's plays as living works of art which can be enjoyed today on stage, film and television in many parts of the world.

CONTENTS

An Elizabethan playhouse. Note the apron stage protruding into the auditorium, the space below it, the inner room at the rear of the stage, the gallery above the inner stage, the canopy over the main stage, and the absence of a roof over the audience.

The Theatre in Shakespeare's Day

On the face of it, the conditions in the Elizabethan theatre were not such as to encourage great writers. The public playhouse itself was not very different from an ordinary inn-yard; it was open to the weather; among the spectators were often louts, pickpockets and prostitutes; some of the actors played up to the rowdy elements in the audience by inserting their own jokes into the authors' lines, while others spoke their words loudly but unfeelingly; the presentation was often rough and noisy, with fireworks to represent storms and battles, and a table and a few chairs to represent a tavern; there were no actresses, so boys took the parts of women, even such subtle and mature ones as Cleopatra and Lady Macbeth; there was rarely any scenery at all in the modern sense. In fact, a quick inspection of the English theatre in the reign of Elizabeth I by a time-traveller from the twentieth century might well produce only one positive reaction: the costumes were often elaborate and beautiful.

Shakespeare himself makes frequent comments in his plays about the limitations of the playhouse and the actors of his time, often apologizing for them. At the beginning of *Henry V* the Prologue refers to the stage as 'this unworthy scaffold' and to the theatre building (the Globe, probably) as 'this wooden O', and emphasizes the urgent need for imagination in making up for all the deficiencies of presentation. In introducing Act IV the Chorus goes so far as to say:

> . . . we shall much disgrace
> With four or five most vile and ragged foils,
> Right ill-dispos'd in brawl ridiculous,
> The name of Agincourt, (lines 49–52)

In *A Midsummer Night's Dream* (Act V, Scene i) he seems to dismiss actors with the words:

The best in this kind are but shadows.

Yet Elizabeth's theatre, with all its faults, stimulated dramatists to a variety of achievement that has never been equalled and, in Shakespeare, produced one of the greatest writers in history. In spite of all his grumbles he seems to have been fascinated by the challenge that it presented him with. It is necessary to re-examine his theatre carefully in order to understand how he was able to achieve so much with the materials he chose to use. What sort of place was the Elizabethan playhouse in reality? What sort of people were these criticized actors? And what sort of audiences gave them their living?

The Development of the Theatre up to Shakespeare's Time

For centuries in England noblemen had employed groups of skilled people to entertain them when required. Under Tudor rule, as England became more secure and united, actors such as these were given more freedom, and they often performed in public, while still acknowledging their 'overlords' (in the 1570s, for example, when Shakespeare was still a schoolboy at Stratford, one famous company was called 'Lord Leicester's Men'). London was rapidly becoming larger and more important in the second half of the sixteenth century, and many of the companies of actors took the opportunities offered to establish themselves at inns on the main roads leading to the City (for example, the Boar's Head in Whitechapel and the Tabard in South-wark) or in the City itself. These groups of actors would come to an agreement with the inn-keeper which would give them the use of the yard for their performances after people had eaten and drunk well in the middle of the day. Before long, some inns were taken over completely by companies of players and thus became the first public theatres. In 1574 the officials of the City of London issued an order which shows clearly that these theatres were both popular and also offensive to some respectable people, because the order complains about 'the inordinate haunting of great multitudes of people, specially youth, to plays interludes and shows; namely occasion of frays and quarrels, evil practices of incontinency in great inns . . .' There is evidence that, on public holidays, the theatres on the banks of the Thames were crowded with noisy apprentices and tradesmen, but it would be wrong to think that audiences were always undiscriminating and loudmouthed. In spite of the disapproval of Puritans and the more staid members of society, by the 1590s, when Shakespeare's plays were beginning to be performed, audiences consisted of a good cross-section of English society, nobility as well as workers, intellectuals as well as simple people out for a laugh; also (and in this respect English theatres were unique in Europe), it was quite normal for respectable women to attend plays. So Shakespeare had to write plays which would appeal to people of widely different kinds. He had to provide 'something for everyone' but at the same time to take care to unify the material so that it would not seem to fall into separate pieces as they watched it. A speech like that of the drunken porter in *Macbeth* could provide the 'groundlings' with a belly-laugh, but also held a deeper significance for those who could appreciate it. The audience he wrote for was one of a number of apparent drawbacks which Shakespeare was able to turn to his and our advantage.

Shakespeare's Actors

Nor were all the actors of the time mere 'rogues, vagabonds and sturdy beggars' as some were described in a Statute of 1572. It is true that many of them had a hard life and earned very little money, but leading actors could become partners in the ownership of the theatres in which they acted: Shakespeare was a shareholder in the Globe and the Blackfriars theatres when he was an actor as well as a playwright. In any case, the attacks made on Elizabethan actors were usually directed at their morals and not at their acting ability; it is clear that many of them must have been good at their trade if they were able to interpret complex works like the great tragedies in such a way as to attract enthusiastic audiences. Undoubtedly some of the boys took the women's parts with skill and confidence, since a man called Coryate, visiting Venice in 1611, expressed surprise that women could act as well as they: 'I saw women act, a thing that I never saw before . . . and they performed it with as good a grace, action, gesture . . . as ever I saw any masculine actor.' The quality of most of the actors who first presented Shakespeare's plays is probably accurately summed up by Fynes Moryson, who wrote, '. . . as there be, in my opinion, more plays in London than in all the parts of the world I have seen, so do these players or comedians excel all other in the world.'

The Structure of the Public Theatre

Although the 'purpose-built' theatres were based on the inn-yards which had been used for play-acting, most of them were circular. The walls contained galleries on three storeys from which the wealthier patrons watched, they must have been something like the 'boxes' in a modern theatre, except that they held much larger numbers – as many as 1500. The 'groundlings' stood on the floor of the building, facing a raised stage which projected from the 'stage-wall', the main features of which were:

1 a small room opening on to the back of the main stage and on the same level as it (rear stage),
2 a gallery above this inner stage (upper stage),
3 canopy projecting from above the gallery over the main stage, to protect the actors from the weather (the 700 or 800 members of the audience who occupied the yard, or 'pit' as we call it today, had the sky above them).

In addition to these features there were dressing-rooms behind the stage and a space underneath it from which entrances could be made through trap-doors. All the acting areas – main stage, rear stage, upper stage and under stage – could be entered by actors directly from their dressing rooms, and all of them were used in productions of Shakespeare's plays. For example, the inner stage, an almost cavelike structure, would have been where Ferdinand and Miranda are 'discovered' playing chess in the last act of *The Tempest*, while the upper stage was certainly the balcony from which Romeo climbs down in Act III of *Romeo and Juliet*.

It can be seen that such a building, simple but adaptable, was not really unsuited to the presentation of plays like Shakespeare's. On the contrary, its simplicity guaranteed the minimum of distraction, while its shape and construction must have produced a sense of involvement on the part of the audience that modern producers would envy.

Other Resources of the Elizabethan Theatre

Although there were few attempts at scenery in the public theatre (painted backcloths were occasionally used in court performances), Shakespeare and his fellow playwrights were able to make use of a fair variety of 'properties', lists of such articles have survived: they include beds, tables, thrones, and also trees, walls, a gallows, a Trojan horse and a 'Mouth of Hell'; in a list of properties belonging to the manager, Philip Henslowe, the curious item 'two mossy banks' appears. Possibly one of them was used for the

> bank whereon the wild thyme blows,
> Where oxlips and the nodding violet grows

in *A Midsummer Night's Dream* (Act II, Scene i). Once again, imagination must have been required of the audience.

Costumes were the one aspect of stage production in which

trouble and expense were hardly ever spared to obtain a magnificent effect. Only occasionally did they attempt any historical accuracy (almost all Elizabethan productions were what we should call 'modern-dress' ones), but they were appropriate to the characters who wore them: kings were seen to be kings and beggars were similarly unmistakable. It is an odd fact that there was usually no attempt at illusion in the costuming: if a costume looked fine and rich it probably was. Indeed, some of the costumes were almost unbelievably expensive. Henslowe lent his company £19 to buy a cloak, and the Alleyn brothers, well-known actors, gave £20 for a 'black velvet cloak, with sleeves embroidered all with silver and gold, lined with black satin striped with gold'.

With the one exception of the costumes, the 'machinery' of the playhouse was economical and uncomplicated rather than crude and rough, as we can see from this second and more leisurely look at it. This meant that playwrights were stimulated to produce the imaginative effects that they wanted from the language that they used. In the case of a really great writer like Shakespeare, when he had learned his trade in the theatre as an actor, it seems that he received quite enough assistance of a mechanical and structural kind without having irksome restrictions and conventions imposed on him; it is interesting to try to guess what he would have done with the highly complex apparatus of a modern television studio. We can see when we look back to his time that he used his instrument, the Elizabethan theatre, to the full, but placed his ultimate reliance on the communication between his imagination and that of his audience through the medium of words. It is, above all, his rich and wonderful use of language that must have made play-going at that time a memorable experience for people of widely different kinds. Fortunately, the deep satisfaction of appreciating and enjoying Shakespeare's work can be ours also, if we are willing to overcome the language difficulty produced by the passing of time.

Shakespeare: A Timeline

Very little indeed is known about Shakespeare's private life; the facts included here are almost the only indisputable ones. The dates of Shakespeare's plays are those on which they were first produced.

1558	Queen Elizabeth crowned.	
1561	Francis Bacon born.	
1564	Christopher Marlowe born.	William Shakespeare born, April 23rd, baptized April 26th.
1566		Shakespeare's brother, Gilbert, born.
1567	Mary, Queen of Scots, deposed. James VI (later James I of England) crowned King of Scotland.	
1572	Ben Jonson born. Lord Leicester's Company (of players) licensed; later called Lord Strange's, then the Lord Chamberlain's and finally (under James) the King's Men.	
1573	John Donne born.	
1574	The Common Council of London directs that all plays and playhouses in London must be licensed.	
1576	James Burbage builds the first public playhouse, The Theatre, at Shoreditch, outside the walls of the City.	
1577	Francis Drake begins his voyage round the world (completed 1580). *Holinshed's Chronicles of England, Scotland and Ireland* published (which	

Shakespeare later used extensively).

1582		Shakespeare married to Anne Hathaway.
1583	The Queen's Company founded by royal warrant.	Shakespeare's daughter, Susanna, born.
1585		Shakespeare's twins, Hamnet and Judith, born.
1586	Sir Philip Sidney, the Elizabethan ideal 'Christian knight', poet, patron, soldier, killed at Zutphen in the Low Countries.	
1587	Mary, Queen of Scots, beheaded. Marlowe's *Tamburlaine (Part I)* first staged.	
1588	Defeat of the Spanish Armada. Marlowe's *Tamburlaine (Part II)* first staged.	
1589	Marlowe's *Jew of Malta* and Kyd's *Spanish Tragedy* (a 'revenge tragedy' and one of the most popular plays of Elizabethan times).	
1590	Spenser's *Faerie Queene* (Books I–III) published.	
1592	Marlowe's *Doctor Faustus* and *Edward II* first staged. Witchcraft trials in Scotland. Robert Greene, a rival playwright, refers to Shakespeare as 'an upstart crow' and 'the only Shake-scene in a country'.	*Titus Andronicus* *Henry VI, Parts I, II and III* *Richard III*
1593	London theatres closed by the plague. Christopher Marlowe killed in a Deptford tavern.	*Two Gentlemen of Verona* *Comedy of Errors* *The Taming of the Shrew* *Love's Labour's Lost*
1594	Shakespeare's company becomes The Lord Chamberlain's Men.	*Romeo and Juliet*

Year	Events	Works
1595	Raleigh's first expedition to Guiana. Last expedition of Drake and Hawkins (both died).	*Richard II* *A Midsummer Night's Dream*
1596	Spenser's *Faerie Queene* (Books IV–VI) published. James Burbage buys rooms at Blackfriars and begins to convert them into a theatre.	*King John* *The Merchant of Venice* Shakespeare's son Hamnet dies. Shakespeare's father is granted a coat of arms.
1597	James Burbage dies, his son Richard, a famous actor, turns the Blackfriars Theatre into a private playhouse.	*Henry IV (Part I)* Shakespeare buys and redecorates New Place at Stratford.
1598	Death of Philip II of Spain	*Henry IV (Part II)* *Much Ado About Nothing*
1599	Death of Edmund Spenser. The Globe Theatre completed at Bankside by Richard and Cuthbert Burbage.	*Henry V* *Julius Caesar* *As You Like It*
1600	Fortune Theatre built at Cripplegate. East India Company founded for the extension of English trade and influence in the East. The Children of the Chapel begin to use the hall at Blackfriars.	*Merry Wives of Windsor* *Troilus and Cressida*
1601		*Hamlet*
1602	Sir Thomas Bodley's library opened at Oxford.	*Twelfth Night*
1603	Death of Queen Elizabeth. James I comes to the throne. Shakespeare's company becomes The King's Men. Raleigh tried, condemned and sent to the Tower	
1604	Treaty of peace with Spain	*Measure for Measure* *Othello* *All's Well that Ends Well*
1605	The Gunpowder Plot: an attempt by a group of Catholics to blow up the Houses of Parliament.	

1606	Guy Fawkes and other plotters executed.	*Macbeth* *King Lear*
1607	Virginia, in America, colonized. A great frost in England.	*Antony and Cleopatra* *Timon of Athens* *Coriolanus* Shakespeare's daughter, Susanna, married to Dr. John Hall.
1608	The company of the Children of the Chapel Royal (who had performed at Blackfriars for ten years) is disbanded. John Milton born. Notorious pirates executed in London.	Richard Burbage leases the Blackfriars Theatre to six of his fellow actors, including Shakespeare. *Pericles, Prince of Tyre*
1609		Shakespeare's Sonnets published.
1610	A great drought in England	*Cymbeline*
1611	Chapman completes his great translation of the *Iliad*, the story of Troy. Authorized Version of the Bible published.	*A Winter's Tale* *The Tempest*
1612	Webster's *The White Devil* first staged.	Shakespeare's brother, Gilbert, dies.
1613	Globe theatre burnt down during a performance of *Henry VIII* (the firing of small cannon set fire to the thatched roof). Webster's *Duchess of Malfi* first staged.	*Henry VIII* *Two Noble Kinsmen* Shakespeare buys a house at Blackfriars.
1614	Globe Theatre rebuilt in 'far finer manner than before'.	
1616	Ben Jonson publishes his plays in one volume. Raleigh released from the Tower in order to prepare an expedition to the gold mines of Guiana.	Shakespeare's daughter, Judith, marries Thomas Quiney. Death of Shakespeare on his birthday, April 23rd.
1618	Raleigh returns to England and is executed on the charge for which he was imprisoned in 1603.	
1623	Publication of the Folio edition of Shakespeare's plays	Death of Anne Shakespeare (née Hathaway).

Life & Times

William Shakespeare the Playwright

There exists a curious paradox when it comes to the life of William Shakespeare. He easily has more words written about him than any other famous English writer, yet we know the least about him. This inevitably means that most of what is written about him is either fabrication or speculation. The reason why so little is known about Shakespeare is that he wasn't a novelist or a historian or a man of letters. He was a playwright, and playwrights were considered fairly low on the social pecking order in Elizabethan society. Writing plays was about providing entertainment for the masses – the great unwashed. It was the equivalent to being a journalist for a tabloid newspaper.

In fact, we only know of Shakespeare's work because two of his friends had the foresight to collect his plays together following his death and have them printed. The only reason they did so was apparently because they rated his talent and thought it would be a shame if his words were lost.

Consequently his body of work has ever since been assessed and reassessed as the greatest contribution to English literature. That is despite the fact that we know that different printers took it upon themselves to heavily edit the material they worked from. We also know that Elizabethan plays were worked and reworked frequently, so that they evolved over time until they were honed to perfection, which means that many different hands played their part in the active writing process. It would therefore be fair to say that any play attributed to Shakespeare is unlikely to contain a great deal of original input. Even the plots were based on well known historical events, so it would be hard to know what fragments of any Shakespeare play came from that single mind.

One might draw a comparison with the Christian bible, which remains such a compelling read because it came from the collaboration of many contributors and translators over centuries, who each adjusted the stories until they could no longer be improved. As virtually nothing is known of Shakespeare's life and even less about his method of working, we shall never know the truth about his plays. They certainly contain some very elegant phrasing, clever plot devices and plenty of words never before seen in print, but as to whether Shakespeare invented them from a unique imagination or whether he simply took them from others around him is anyone's guess.

The best bet seems to be that Shakespeare probably took the lead role in devising the original drafts of the plays, but was open to collaboration from any source when it came to developing them into workable scripts for effective performances. He would have had to work closely with his fellow actors in rehearsals, thereby finding out where to edit, abridge, alter, reword and so on.

In turn, similar adjustments would have occurred in his absence, so that definitive versions of his plays never really existed. In effect Shakespeare was only responsible for providing the framework of plays, upon which others took liberties over time. This wasn't helped by the fact that the English language itself was not definitive at that time either. The consequence was that people took it upon themselves to spell words however they pleased or to completely change words and phrasing to suit their own preferences.

It is easy to see then, that Shakespeare's plays were always going to have lives of their own, mutating and distorting in detail like Chinese whispers. The culture of creative preservation was simply not established in Elizabethan England. Creative ownership of Shakespeare's plays was lost to him as soon as he released them into the consciousness of others. They saw nothing wrong with taking his ideas and running with them, because no one had ever suggested that one shouldn't, and Shakespeare probably regarded his work in the same way. His plays weren't sacrosanct works of art, they were templates for theatre folk to make their livings from, so they had every right to mould them into productions that drew in the crowds as effectively as possible. Shakespeare was like the helmsman of a sailing ship, steering the vessel but wholly reliant on the team work of his crew to arrive at the desired destination.

It seems that Shakespeare certainly had a natural gift, but the genius of his plays may be attributable to the collective efforts of Shakespeare and others. It is a rather satisfying notion to think that *his* plays might actually be the creative outpourings of the Elizabethan milieu in which Shakespeare immersed himself. That makes them important social documents as well as seminal works of the English language.

Money in Shakespeare's Day

It is extremely difficult, if not impossible, to relate the value of money in our time to its value in another age and to compare prices of commodities today and in the past. Many items *are* simply not comparable on grounds of quality or serviceability.

There was a bewildering variety of coins in use in Elizabethan England. As nearly all English and European coins were gold or silver, they had intrinsic value apart from their official value. This meant that foreign coins circulated freely in England and were officially recognized, for example the French crown (écu) worth about 30p (72 cents), and the Spanish ducat worth about 33p (79 cents). The following table shows some of the coins mentioned by Shakespeare and their relation to one another.

GOLD	British	American	SILVER	British	American
sovereign (heavy type)	£1.50	$3.60	shilling	10p	24c
sovereign (light type)	66p–£l	$1.58–$2.40	groat	1.5p	4c
angel					
royal	33p–50p	79c–$1.20			
noble	50p	$1.20			
crown	25p	60c			

A comparison of the following prices in Shakespeare's time with the prices of the same items today will give some idea of the change in the value of money.

ITEM	PRICE British	American	ITEM	PRICE British	American
beef, per lb.	0.5p	1c	cherries (lb.)	1p	2c
mutton, leg	7.5p	18c	7 oranges	1p	2c
rabbit	3.5p	9c	1 lemon	1p	2c
chicken	3p	8c	cream (quart)	2.5p	6c
potatoes (lb)	10p	24c	sugar (lb.)	£1	$2.40
carrots (bunch)	1p	2c	sack (wine) (gallon)	14p	34c
8 artichokes	4p	9c	tobacco (oz.)	25p	60c
1 cucumber	1p	2c	biscuits (lb.)	12.5p	30c

INTRODUCTION

To use an operatic analogy, *Richard II* stands to its sequels *Henry IV* and *Henry V* as a kind of overture, in which all the major themes are deployed and their development and resolution anticipated. Economical, lucid and open-textured, yet also coolly ironical, *Richard II* is to its young author's so-called second tetralogy what the mature Wagner's *Rhinegold* was to *The Ring*. As in *Rhinegold* the protagonists are mostly rather unsympathetic. This might be thought *Richard II*'s only serious dramatic weakness. But we may surely discount that as simply the price of the play's great virtues: its matchlessly acute observation and its wholly unsentimental realism concerning the crucial political questions of power, legitimacy and authority.

The play focuses with unusual intentness on the hereditary monarch's supposed divine right to unconditional obedience, irrespective of his actual fitness to rule. As a self-conscious theory, this seemingly ultra-traditionalist doctrine was in fact fairly new, and was far more vigorously promoted by the modernising and centralising Tudors and Stuarts than by their feudal predecessors. For traditionally, as Lord Chief Justice Coke pointed out to an unamused James I, the king was subject not only to God, but also to the laws and customs of his people, whose figurehead and representative he was.

Shakespeare seems sympathetic to this older view, which now seems more modern than its rival. Unlike Richard, a wise ruler, if he wants his laws to be obeyed, will surely try to be seen observing them himself. Richard's downfall is due partly to chance (he and his army are in Ireland when Bolingbroke invades), but mostly to his own childlike defects of character, his vanity and frivolity. These lead him first into extravagance and bankruptcy, thence to extortion, and finally to his barefaced seizure of Bolingbroke's inheritance. He almost wilfully alienates the jealous feudal nobility, helping himself to their goods, entrusting his offices to upstarts and parasites, and compromising the majesty of state (whence the nobility derives its lustre) by selling Crown revenues as if they were his alone to dispose of.

His fecklessness and arrogance, his manic oscillation between vainglory and self-pity, his invariable propensity to strike fantastic theatrical poses rather than face up to reality; above all, his obsessive, near-magical conviction that his divine right automatically guarantees him God's protection from the inevitable consequences of his folly and incompetence; all ensure that he learns nothing from experience until everything is irrevocably lost. Only when, tragically and far too late, he awakens to the truth about himself are we finally moved to sympathy and, struck by his unexpected courage in confronting his assassins, even to admiration.

By contrast with Richard, Henry Bolingbroke has everything a ruler needs except a title (though as his henchman Northumberland stresses, he is Richard's near kinsman). Popular and robustly patriotic, as the effete Richard is not, he is equally not short of the requisite deviousness, hypocrisy and ruthlessness. Never fully admitting, even to himself, the real reason for his return from banishment, though he has set sail for England even before learning of his dispossession, he more or less sleepwalks to the throne. Indeed, as both he and Richard recognise, the throne is effectively his from the instant that the helpless king is forced to acquiesce in his initial disobedience.

At least in the short run, and as Marvell later pointed out in his *Horatian Ode*, power won by force can only be maintained by force. The second tetralogy consistently demonstrates how true civil peace can be the product of neither force, nor virtue, nor law, nor myth taken singly, but only of all four together, and that when a successful usurper flouts one myth (hereditary right, say), he is constrained, if he hopes ever to rule by consent, to manu-facture another.

The simplest alternative myth, hit upon independently by both Bolingbroke and the conscience-stricken defector York, is that success might in itself be evidence of God's approval and assistance. Unfortunately many of Henry's supporters, especially the self-seeking, deeply unattractive Northumberland, rather ascribe his victory to their own efforts, and accordingly, in *Henry IV*, reckon themselves hard done by in the division of the spoils. It is left to Bolingbroke's son, Henry V, to secure national unity by the most drastic and Machiavellian of expedients, viz. declaring unprovoked war on a neighbour, twisting the Church's arm to get it declared a crusade, leading it in person, and (perhaps most important of all) coming within an ace of defeat.

In such a world of disingenuousness, the deep chivalric pieties of John of Gaunt and the unfortunate Mowbray, already reduced to irrelevance by Richard's shamelessly cynical dismissal or exploitation of them, seem like mere fragrant memories of a vanished innocence. The honour which triumphs at Agincourt alongside a new populist and pragmatic conception of legitimacy is an altogether less rarefied affair.

LIST OF CHARACTERS

King Richard The Second

John Of Gaunt	Duke of Lancaster,
Edmund Of Langley	Duke of York, uncles to the King
Henry surnamed *Bolingbroke*	Duke of Hereford, son of John of Gaunt, afterwards King Henry IV
Duke Of Aumerle	son of the Duke of York
Thomas Mowbray	Duke of Norfolk
Duke Of Surrey	
Earl Of Salisbury	
Earl Berkeley	
Bushy, Bagot, Green	favourites of King Richard
Earl Of Northumberland	
Henry Percy surnamed *Hotspur*	his son
Lord Ross	
Lord Willoughby	
Lord Fitzwater	
Bishop Of Carlisle	
Abbot Of Westminster	
Lord Marshal	
Sir Stephen Scroop	
Sir Pierce Of Exton	Captain of a band of Welshmen
Two Gardeners	
Queen	to King Richard
Duchess Of York	
Duchess Of Gloucester	widow of Thomas of Woodstock

Duke of Gloucester, Lady attending on the Queen, Lords, Heralds, Officers, Soldiers, a Keeper, a Messenger, a Groom, and *other Attendants*

The Scene: England And Wales.

ACT ONE
Scene I

London. The palace.

[Enter KING RICHARD, JOHN OF GAUNT, with other Nobles and Attendants.]

King Richard
Old John of Gaunt, time-honoured Lancaster,
Hast thou, according to thy oath and band,
Brought hither Henry Hereford, thy bold son,
Here to make good the boist'rous late appeal,
Which then our leisure would not let us hear,   5
Against the Duke of Norfolk, Thomas Mowbray?

Gaunt
I have, my liege.

King Richard
Tell me, moreover, hast thou sounded him
If he appeal the Duke on ancient malice,
Or worthily, as a good subject should,   10
On some known ground of treachery in him?

Gaunt
As near as I could sift him on that argument,
On some apparent danger seen in him
Aim'd at your Highness – no inveterate malice.

King Richard
Then call them to our presence: face to face   15
And frowning brow to brow, ourselves will hear
The accuser and the accused freely speak.
High-stomach'd are they both and full of ire,
In rage, deaf as the sea, hasty as fire.

[Enter BOLINGBROKE and MOWBRAY.]

Bolingbroke
Many years of happy days befall My gracious   20

sovereign, my most loving liege!

Mowbray

Each day still better other's happiness
Until the heavens, envying earth's good hap,
Add an immortal title to your crown!

King Richard

25 We thank you both; yet one but flatters us,
As well appeareth by the cause you come;
Namely, to appeal each other of high treason.
Cousin of Hereford, what dost thou object
Against the Duke of Norfolk, Thomas Mowbray?

Bolingbroke

30 First – heaven be the record to my speech!
In the devotion of a subject's love,
Tend'ring the precious safety of my prince,
And free from other misbegotten hate,
Come I appellant to this princely presence.

35 Now, Thomas Mowbray, do I turn to thee,
And mark my greeting well; for what I speak
My body shall make good upon this earth,
Or my divine soul answer it in heaven –
Thou art a traitor and a miscreant,

40 Too good to be so, and too bad to live,
Since the more fair and crystal is the sky,
The uglier seem the clouds that in it fly.
Once more, the more to aggravate the note,
With a foul traitor's name stuff I thy throat;

45 And wish – so please my sovereign – ere I move,
What my tongue speaks, my right drawn sword may
prove.

Mowbray

Let not my cold words here accuse my zeal.
'Tis not the trial of a woman's war,
The bitter clamour of two eager tongues,

50 Can arbitrate this cause betwixt us twain;
The blood is hot that must be cool'd for this.
Yet can I not of such tame patience boast

As to be hush'd and nought at all to say.
First, the fair reverence of your Highness curbs me
From giving reins and spurs to my free speech; 55
Which else would post until it had return'd
These terms of treason doubled down his throat.
Setting aside his blood's royalty,
And let him be no kinsman to my liege,
I do defy him, and I spit at him, 60
Call him a slanderous coward and a villain;
Which to maintain, I would allow him odds
And meet him, were I tied to run afoot
Even to the frozen ridges of the Alps,
Or any other ground inhabitable 65
Where ever Englishman durst set his foot.
Meantime let this defend my loyalty –
By all my hopes, most falsely doth he lie.

Bolingbroke

Pale trembling coward, there I throw my gage,
Disclaiming here the kindred of the King; 70
And lay aside my high blood's royalty,
Which fear, not reverence, makes thee to except.
If guilty dread have left thee so much strength
As to take up mine honour's pawn, then stoop.
By that and all the rites of knighthood else 75
Will I make good against thee, arm to arm,
What I have spoke or thou canst worse devise.

Mowbray

I take it up; and by that sword I swear
Which gently laid my knighthood on my shoulder
I'll answer thee in any fair degree 80
Or chivalrous design of knightly trial;
And when I mount, alive may I not light
If I be traitor or unjustly fight!

King Richard

What doth our cousin lay to Mowbray's charge?
It must be great that can inherit us 85
So much as of a thought of ill in him.

Bolingbroke
> Look what I speak, my life shall prove it true –
> That Mowbray hath receiv'd eight thousand nobles
> In name of lendings for your Highness' soldiers,
90   The which he hath detain'd for lewd employments
> Like a false traitor and injurious villain.
> Besides, I say and will in battle prove –
> Or here, or elsewhere to the furthest verge
> That ever was survey'd by English eye –
95   That all the treasons for these eighteen years
> Complotted and contrived in this land
> Fetch from false Mowbray their first head and
>   spring.
> Further I say, and further will maintain
> Upon his bad life to make all this good,
100 That he did plot the Duke of Gloucester's death,
> Suggest his soon-believing adversaries,
> And consequently, like a traitor coward,
> Sluic'd out his innocent soul through streams of
>   blood;
> Which blood, like sacrificing Abel's, cries,
105 Even from the tongueless caverns of the earth,
> To me for justice and rough chastisement;
> And, by the glorious worth of my descent,
> This arm shall do it, or this life be spent.

King Richard
> How high a pitch his resolution soars!
110 Thomas of Norfolk, what say'st thou to this?

Mowbray
> O, let my sovereign turn away his face
> And bid his ears a little while be deaf,
> Till I have told this slander of his blood
> How God and good men hate so foul a liar.

King Richard
115 Mowbray, impartial are our eyes and ears.
> Were he my brother, nay, my kingdom's heir,
> As he is but my father's brother's son,

Now by my sceptre's awe I make a vow,
Such neighbour nearness to our sacred blood
Should nothing privilege him nor partialize   120
The unstooping firmness of my upright soul.
He is our subject, Mowbray; so art thou:
Free speech and fearless I to thee allow.

Mowbray
Then, Bolingbroke, as low as to thy heart,
Through the false passage of thy throat, thou liest.   125
Three parts of that receipt I had for Calais
Disburs'd I duly to his Highness' soldiers;
The other part reserv'd I by consent,
For that my sovereign liege was in my debt
Upon remainder of a dear account   130
Since last I went to France to fetch his queen:
Now swallow down that lie. For Gloucester's death –
I slew him not, but to my own disgrace
Neglected my sworn duty in that case.
For you, my noble Lord of Lancaster,   135
The honourable father to my foe,
Once did I lay an ambush for your life,
A trespass that doth vex my grieved soul;
But ere I last receiv'd the sacrament
I did confess it, and exactly begg'd   140
Your Grace's pardon; and I hope I had it.
This is my fault. As for the rest appeal'd,
It issues from the rancour of a villain,
A recreant and most degenerate traitor;
Which in myself I boldly will defend,   145
And interchangeably hurl down my gage
Upon this overweening traitor's foot
To prove myself a loyal gentleman
Even in the best blood chamber'd in his bosom.
In haste whereof, most heartily I pray   150
Your Highness to assign our trial day.

King Richard
Wrath-kindled gentlemen, be rul'd by me;

Let's purge this choler without letting blood –
This we prescribe, though no physician;
155   Deep malice makes too deep incision.
Forget, forgive; conclude and be agreed:
Our doctors say this is no month to bleed.
Good uncle, let this end where it begun,
We'll calm the Duke of Norfolk, you your son.

Gaunt
160   To be a make-peace shall become my age.
Throw down, my son, the Duke of Norfolk's gage.

King Richard
And, Norfolk, throw down his.

Gaunt
                        When, Harry, when?
Obedience bids I should not bid again.

King Richard
Norfolk, throw down; we bid. There is no boot.

Mowbray
165   Myself I throw, dread sovereign, at thy foot;
My life thou shalt command, but not my shame:
The one my duty owes; but my fair name,
Despite of death, that lives upon my grave
To dark dishonour's use thou shalt not have.
170   I am disgrac'd, impeach'd, and baffl'd here;
Pierc'd to the soul with slander's venom'd spear,
The which no balm can cure but his heartblood
Which breath'd this poison.

King Richard
                      Rage must be withstood:
Give me his gage – lions make leopards tame.

Mowbray
175   Yea, but not change his spots. Take but my shame,
And I resign my gage. My dear dear lord,
The purest treasure mortal times afford
Is spotless reputation; that away,
Men are but gilded loam or painted caly.
180   A jewel in a ten-times barr'd-up chest

Is a bold spirit in a loyal breast.
Mine honour is my life; both grow in one;
Take honour from me, and my life is done:
Then, dear my liege, mine honour let me try;
In that I live, and for that will I die.   185

King Richard
Cousin, throw up your gage; do you begin.

Bolingbroke
O, God defend my soul from such deep sin!
Shall I seem crest-fallen in my father's sight?
Or with pale beggar-fear impeach my height
Before this outdar'd dastard? Ere my tongue   190
Shall wound my honour with such feeble wrong
Or sound so base a parle, my teeth shall tear
The slavish motive of recanting fear,
And spit it bleeding in his high disgrace,
Where shame doth harbour, even in Mowbray's face. 195

[Exit GAUNT.*]*

King Richard
We were not born to sue, but to command;
Which since we cannot do to make you friends,
Be ready, as your lives shall answer it,
At Coventry, upon Saint Lambert's day.
There shall your swords and lances arbitrate   200
The swelling difference of your settled hate;
Since we can not atone you, we shall see
Justice design the victor's chivalry.
Lord Marshal, command our officers-at-arms
Be ready to direct these home alarms.   205

[Exeunt.]

Scene II

London. The Duke of Lancaster's palace.

[*Enter* JOHN OF GAUNT *with the* DUCHESS OF GLOUCESTER.]

Gaunt
    Alas, the part I had in Woodstock's blood
    Doth more solicit me than your exclaims
    To stir against the butchers of his life!
    But since correction lieth in those hands
5   Which made the fault that we cannot correct,
    Put we our quarrel to the will of heaven;
    Who, when they see the hours ripe on earth,
    Will rain hot vengeance on offenders' heads.

Duchess
    Finds brotherhood in thee no sharper spur?
10   Hath love in thy old blood no living fire?
    Edward's seven sons, where of thyself art one,
    Were as seven vials of his sacred blood,
    Or seven fair branches springing from one root.
    Some of those seven are dried by nature's course,
15   Some of those branches by the Destinies cut;
    But Thomas, my dear lord, my life, my Gloucester,
    One vial full of Edward's sacred blood,
    One flourishing branch of his most royal root,
    Is crack'd, and all the precious liquor spilt;
20   Is hack'd down, and his summer leaves all faded,
    By envy's hand and murder's bloody axe.
    Ah, Gaunt, his blood was thine! That bed, that womb,
    That mettle, that self mould, that fashion'd thee,
    Made him a man; and though thou livest and breathest,
25   Yet art thou slain in him. Thou dost consent

In some large measure to thy father's death
In that thou seest thy wretched brother die,
Who was the model of thy father's life.
Call it not patience, Gaunt – it is despair;
In suff'ring thus thy brother to be slaught'red, 30
Thou showest the naked pathway to thy life,
Teaching stern murder how to butcher thee.
That which in mean men we entitle patience
Is pale cold cowardice in noble breasts.
What shall I say? To safeguard thine own life 35
The best way is to venge my Gloucester's death.

Gaunt

God's is the quarrel; for God's substitute,
His deputy anointed in His sight,
Hath caus'd his death; the which if wrongfully,
Let heaven revenge; for I may never lift 40
An angry arm against His minister.

Duchess

Where then, alas, may I complain myself?

Gaunt

To God, the widow's champion and defence.

Duchess

Why then I will. Farewell, old Gaunt.
Thou goest to Coventry, there to behold 45
Our cousin Hereford and fell Mowbray fight.
O, sit my husband's wrongs on Hereford's spear,
That it may enter butcher Mowbray's breast!
Or, if misfortune miss the first career,
Be Mowbray's sins so heavy in his bosom 50
That they may break his foaming courser's back
And throw the rider headlong in the lists,
A caitiff recreant to my cousin Hereford!
Farewell, old Gaunt; thy sometimes brother's wife,
With her companion, Grief, must end her life. 55

Gaunt

Sister, farewell; I must to Coventry.
As much good stay with thee as go with me!

Duchess
Yet one word more – grief boundeth where it falls,
Not with the empty hollowness, but weight.
60 I take my leave before I have begun,
For sorrow ends not when it seemeth done.
Commend me to thy brother, Edmund York.
Lo, this is all – nay, yet depart not so;
Though this be all, do not so quickly go;
65 I shall remember more. Bid him – ah, what? –
With all good speed at Plashy visit me.
Alack, and what shall good old York there see
But empty lodgings and unfurnish'd walls,
Unpeopled offices, untrodden stones?
70 And what hear there for welcome but my groans?
Therefore commend me; let him not come there
To seek out sorrow that dwells every where.
Desolate, desolate, will I hence and die;
The last leave of thee takes my weeping eye.

[Exeunt.]

Scene III

The lists at Coventry.

[Enter the LORD MARSHAL *and the* DUKE OF AUMERLE.*]*

Marshal
My Lord Aumerle, is Harry Hereford arm'd?
Aumerle
Yea, at all points; and longs to enter in.
Marshal
The Duke of Norfolk, sprightfully and bold,
Stays but the summons of the appellant's trumpet.
Aumerle
Why then, the champions are prepar'd, and stay   5
For nothing but his Majesty's approach.

[The trumpets sound, and the KING *enters with his*
nobles, GAUNT, BUSHY, BAGOT, GREEN, *and Others.*
When they are set, enter MOWBRAY, DUKE OF
NORFOLK, *in arms, defendant, and a Herald.]*

King Richard
Marshal, demand of yonder champion
The cause of his arrival here in arms;
Ask him his name; and orderly proceed
To swear him in the justice of his cause.   10
Marshal
In God's name and the King's, say who thou art,
And why thou comest thus knightly clad in arms;
Against what man thou com'st, and what thy
    quarrel.
Speak truly on thy knighthood and thy oath;
As so defend thee heaven and thy valour!   15
Mowbray
My name is Thomas Mowbray, Duke of Norfolk;
Who hither come engaged by my oath –
Which God defend a knight should violate! –
Both to defend my loyalty and truth

20 To God, my King, and my succeeding issue,
   Against the Duke of Hereford that appeals me;
   And, by the grace of God and this mine arm,
   To prove him, in defending of myself,
   A traitor to my God, my King, and me.
25 And as I truly fight, defend me heaven!

[The trumpets sound. Enter BOLINGBROKE, DUKE OF
HEREFORD, *appellant, in armour, and a Herald.]*

King Richard
   Marshal, ask yonder knight in arms,
   Both who he is and why he cometh hither
   Thus plated in habiliments of war;
   And formally, according to our law,
30 Depose him in the justice of his cause.
Marshal
   What is thy name? and wherefore com'st thou
      hither
   Before King Richard in his royal lists?
   Against whom comest thou? and what's thy quarrel?
   Speak like a true knight, so defend thee heaven!
Bolingbroke
35 Harry of Hereford, Lancaster, and Derby,
   Am I; who ready here do stand in arms
   To prove, by God's grace and my body's valour,
   In lists on Thomas Mowbray, Duke of Norfolk,
   That he is a traitor, foul and dangerous,
40 To God of heaven, King Richard, and to me.
   And as I truly fight, defend me heaven!
Marshal
   On pain of death, no person be so bold
   Or daring-hardy as to touch the lists,
   Except the Marshal and such officers
45 Appointed to direct these fair designs.
Bolingbroke
   Lord Marshal, let me kiss my sovereign's hand,
   And bow my knee before his Majesty;

For Mowbray and myself are like two men
That vow a long and weary pilgrimage.
Then let us take a ceremonious leave   50
And loving farewell of our several friends.

Marshal

The appellant in all duty greets your Highness,
And craves to kiss your hand and take his leave.

King Richard

We will descend and fold him in our arms.
Cousin of Hereford, as thy cause is right,   55
So be thy fortune in this royal fight!
Farewell, my blood; which if to-day thou shed,
Lament we may, but not revenge thee dead.

Bolingbroke

O, let no noble eye profane a tear
For me, if I be gor'd with Mowbray's spear.   60
As confident as is the falcon's flight
Against a bird, do I with Mowbray fight.
My loving lord, I take my leave of you;
Of you, my noble cousin, Lord Aumerle;
Not sick, although I have to do with death,   65
But lusty, young, and cheerly drawing breath.
Lo, as at English feasts, so I regreet
The daintiest last, to make the end most sweet.
O thou, the earthly author of my blood,
Whose youthful spirit, in me regenerate,   70
Doth with a twofold vigour lift me up
To reach at victory above my head,
Add proof unto mine armour with thy prayers,
And with thy blessings steel my lance's point,
That it may enter Mowbray's waxen coat   75
And furbish new the name of John o' Gaunt,
Even in the lusty haviour of his son.

Gaunt

God in thy good cause make thee prosperous!
Be swift like lightning in the execution,
And let thy blows, doubly redoubled,   80

Fall like amazing thunder on the casque
Of thy adverse pernicious enemy.
Rouse up thy youthful blood, be valiant, and live.

Bolingbroke
Mine innocence and Saint George to thrive!

Mowbray
85   However God or fortune cast my lot,
There lives or dies, true to King Richard's throne,
A loyal, just, and upright gentleman.
Never did captive with a freer heart
Cast off his chains of bondage, and embrace
90   His golden uncontroll'd enfranchisement,
More than my dancing soul doth celebrate
This feast of battle with mine adversary.
Most mighty liege, and my companion peers,
Take from my mouth the wish of happy years.
95   As gentle and as jocund as to jest
Go I to fight: truth hath a quiet breast.

King Richard
Farewell, my lord, securely I espy
Virtue with valour couched in thine eye.
Order the trial, Marshal, and begin.

Marshal
100   Harry of Hereford, Lancaster, and Derby,
Receive thy lance; and God defend the right!

Bolingbroke
Strong as a tower in hope, I cry amen.

Marshal
[*To an Officer*] Go bear this lance to Thomas, Duke of
    Norfolk.

1Herald
Harry of Hereford, Lancaster, and Derby,
105   Stands here for God, his sovereign, and himself,
On pain to be found false and recreant,
To prove the Duke of Norfolk, Thomas Mowbray,
A traitor to his God, his King, and him;
And dares him to set forward to the fight.

2 Herald

Here standeth Thomas Mowbray, Duke of Norfolk, 110
On pain to be found false and recreant,
Both to defend himself, and to approve
Henry of Hereford, Lancaster, and Derby,
To God, his sovereign, and to him disloyal,
Courageously and with a free desire 115
Attending but the signal to begin.

Marshal

Sound trumpets; and set forward, combatants.
[*A charge sounded.*]
Stay, the King hath thrown his warder down.

King Richard

Let them lay by their helmets and their spears,
And both return back to their chairs again. 120
Withdraw with us; and let the trumpets sound
While we return these dukes what we decree.

[*A long flourish, while the* KING *consults his Council.*]

Draw near,
And list what with our council we have done.
For that our kindgom's earth should not be soil'd 125
With that dear blood which it hath fostered;
And for our eyes do hate the dire aspect
Of civil wounds plough'd up with neighbours'
    sword;
And for we think the eagle-winged pride
Of sky-aspiring and ambitious thoughts, 130
With rival-hating envy, set on you
To wake our peace, which in our country's cradle
Draws the sweet infant breath of gentle sleep;
Which so rous'd up with boist'rous untun'd drums,
With harsh-resounding trumpet's dreadful bray, 135
And grating shock of wrathful iron arms,
Might from our quiet confines fright fair peace
And make us wade even in our kindred's blood –
Therefore we banish you our territories.

140   You, cousin Hereford, upon pain of life,
        Till twice five summers have enrich'd our fields
        Shall not regreet our fair dominions,
        But tread the stranger paths of banishment.

    Bolingbroke
        Your will be done. This must my comfort be –

145   That sun that warms you here shall shine on me,
        And those his golden beams to you here lent
        Shall point on me and gild my banishment.

    King Richard
        Norfolk, for thee remains a heavier doom,
        Which I with some unwillingness pronounce:

150   The sly slow hours shall not determinate
        The dateless limit of thy dear exile;
        The hopeless word of 'never to return'
        Breathe I against thee, upon pain of life.

    Mowbray
        A heavy sentence, my most sovereign liege,

155   And all unlook'd for from your Highness' mouth.
        A dearer merit, not so deep a maim
        As to be cast forth in the common air,
        Have I deserved at your Highness' hands.
        The language I have learnt these forty years,

160   My native English, now I must forgo;
        And now my tongue's use is to me no more
        Than an unstringed viol or a harp;
        Or like a cunning instrument cas'd up
        Or, being open, put into his hands

165   That knows no touch to tune the harmony.
        Within my mouth you have engaol'd my tongue,
        Doubly portcullis'd with my teeth and lips;
        And dull, unfeeling, barren ignorance
        Is made my gaoler to attend on me.

170   I am too old to fawn upon a nurse,
        Too far in years to be a pupil now.
        What is thy sentence, then, but speechless death,
        Which robs my tongue from breathing native breath?

King Richard
> It boots thee not to be compassionate;
> After our sentence plaining comes too late.   175
Mowbray
> Then thus I turn me from my country's light,
> To dwell in solemn shades of endless night.
King Richard
> Return again, and take an oath with thee.
> Lay on our royal sword your banish'd hands;
> Swear by the duty that you owe to God,   180
> Our part therein we banish with yourselves,
> To keep the oath that we administer:
> You never shall, so help you truth and God,
> Embrace each other's love in banishment;
> Nor never look upon each other's face;   185
> Nor never write, regreet, nor reconcile
> This louring tempest of your home-bred hate;
> Nor never by advised purpose meet
> To plot, contrive, or complot any ill,
> 'Gainst us, our state, our subjects, or our land.   190
Bolingbroke
> I swear.
Mowbray
> And I, to keep all this.
Bolingbroke
> Norfolk, so far as to mine enemy:
> By this time, had the King permitted us,
> One of our souls had wand'red in the air,   195
> Banish'd this frail sepulchre of our flesh,
> As now our flesh is banish'd from this land –
> Confess thy treasons ere thou fly the realm;
> Since thou hast far to go, bear not along
> The clogging burden of a guilty soul.   200
Mowbray
> No, Bolingbroke; if ever I were traitor,
> My name be blotted from the book of life,
> And I from heaven banish'd as from hence!

But what thou art, God, thou, and I, do know;
205   And all too soon, I fear, the King shall rue.
Farewell, my liege. Now no way can I stray:
Save back to England, all the world's my way.

[Exit.]

King Richard
Uncle, even in the glasses of thine eyes
I see thy grieved heart. Thy sad aspect
210   Hath from the number of his banish'd years
Pluck'd four away. *[To* BOLINGBROKE*]* Six frozen
    winters spent,
Return with welcome home from banishment.
Bolingbroke
How long a time lies in one little word!
Four lagging winters and four wanton springs
215   End in a word: such is the breath of Kings.
Gaunt
I thank my liege that in regard of me
He shortens four years of my son's exile;
But little vantage shall I reap thereby,
For ere the six years that he hath to spend
220   Can change their moons and bring their times about,
My oil-dried lamp and time-bewasted light
Shall be extinct with age and endless night;
My inch of taper will be burnt and done,
And blindfold death not let me see my son.
King Richard
225   Why, uncle, thou hast many years to live.
Gaunt
But not a minute, King, that thou canst give:
Shorten my days thou canst with sullen sorrow
And pluck nights from me, but not lend a morrow;
Thou canst help time to furrow me with age,
230   But stop no wrinkle in his pilgrimage;
Thy word is current with him for my death,
But dead, thy kingdom cannot buy my breath.

King Richard

    Thy son is banish'd upon good advice,

    Whereto thy tongue a party-verdict gave.

    Why at our justice seem'st thou then to lour?   235

Gaunt

    Things sweet to taste prove in digestion sour.

    You urg'd me as a judge; but I had rather

    You would have bid me argue like a father.

    O, had it been a stranger, not my child,

    To smooth his fault I should have been more mild.   240

    A partial slander sought I to avoid,

    And in the sentence my own life destroy'd.

    Alas, I look'd when some of you should say

    I was too strict to make mine own away;

    But you gave leave to my unwilling tongue   245

    Against my will to do myself this wrong.

King Richard

    Cousin, farewell; and, uncle, bid him so.

    Six years we banish him, and he shall go.

[Flourish. Exit KING *with train.]*

Aumerle

    Cousin, farewell; what presence must not know,

    From where you do remain let paper show.   250

Marshal

    My lord, no leave take I, for I will ride

    As far as land will let me by your side.

Gaunt

    O, to what purpose dost thou hoard thy words,

    That thou returnest no greeting to thy friends?

Bolingbroke

    I have too few to take my leave of you,   255

    When the tongue's office should be prodigal

    To breathe the abundant dolour of the heart.

Gaunt

    Thy grief is but thy absence for a time.

Bolingbroke
Joy absent, grief is present for that time.
Gaunt
260   What is six winters? They are quickly gone.
Bolingbroke
To men in joy; but grief makes one hour ten.
Gaunt
Call it a travel that thou tak'st for pleasure.
Bolingbroke
My heart will sigh when I miscall it so,
Which finds it an enforced pilgrimage.
Gaunt
265   The sullen passage of thy weary steps
Esteem as foil wherein thou art to set
The precious jewel of thy home return.
Bolingbroke
Nay, rather, every tedious stride I make
Will but remember me what a deal of world
270   I wander from the jewels that I love.
Must I not serve a long apprenticehood
To foreign passages; and in the end,
Having my freedom, boast of nothing else
But that I was a journeyman to grief?
Gaunt
275   All places that the eye of heaven visits
Are to a wise man ports and happy havens.
Teach thy necessity to reason thus:
There is no virtue like necessity.
Think not the King did banish thee,
280   But thou the King. Woe doth the heavier sit
Where it perceives it is but faintly borne.
Go, say I sent thee forth to purchase honour,
And not the King exil'd thee; or suppose
Devouring pestilence hangs in our air
285   And thou art flying to a fresher clime.
Look what thy soul holds dear, imagine it
To lie that way thou goest, not whence thou com'st.

Suppose the singing birds musicians,
The grass whereon thou tread'st the presence
   strew'd,
The flowers fair ladies, and thy steps no more   290
Than a delightful measure or a dance;
For gnarling sorrow hath less power to bite
The man that mocks at it and sets it light.

Bolingbroke

O, who can hold a fire in his hand
By thinking on the frosty Caucasus?   295
Or cloy the hungry edge of appetite
By bare imagination of a feast?
Or wallow naked in December snow
By thinking on fantastic summer's heat?
O, no! the apprehension of the good   300
Gives but the greater feeling to the worse.
Fell sorrow's tooth doth never rankle more
Than when he bites, but lanceth not the sore.

Gaunt

Come, come, my son, I'll bring thee on thy way.
Had I thy youth and cause, I would not stay.   305

Bolingbroke

Then, England's ground, farewell; sweet soil, adieu;
My mother, and my nurse, that bears me yet!
Where'er I wander, boast of this I can:
Though banish'd, yet a trueborn English man.

[Exeunt.]

Scene IV

London. The court.

[Enter the KING, *with* BAGOT *and* GREEN, *at one door;
and the* DUKE OF AUMERLE *at another.]*

King Richard
>   We did observe. Cousin Aumerle, How far brought you
>   high Hereford on his way?

Aumerle
>   I brought high Hereford, if you call him so,
>   But to the next high way, and there I left him.

King Richard
5   And say, what store of parting tears were shed?

Aumerle
>   Faith, none for me; except the northeast wind,
>   Which then blew bitterly against our faces,
>   Awak'd the sleeping rheum, and so by chance
>   Did grace our hollow parting with a tear.

King Richard
10   What said our cousin when you parted with him?

Aumerle
>   'Farewell.'
>   And, for my heart disdained that my tongue
>   Should so profane the word, that taught me craft
>   To counterfeit oppression of such grief
15   That words seem'd buried in my sorrow's grave.
>   Marry, would the word 'farewell' have length'ned
>   hours
>   And added years to his short banishment,
>   He should have had a volume of farewells;
>   But since it would not, he had none of me.

King Richard
20   He is our cousin, cousin; but 'tis doubt,
>   When time shall call him home from banishment,
>   Whether our kinsman come to see his friends.
>   Ourself, and Bushy, Bagot here, and Green,

Observ'd his courtship to the common people;
How he did seem to dive into their hearts   25
With humble and familiar courtesy;
What reverence he did throw away on slaves,
Wooing poor craftsmen with the craft of smiles
And patient underbearing of his fortune,
As 'twere to banish their affects with him.   30
Off goes his bonnet to an oyster-wench;
A brace of draymen bid God speed him well
And had the tribute of his supple knee,
With 'Thanks, my countrymen, my loving friends';
As were our England in reversion his,   35
And he our subjects' next degree in hope.

Green

Well, he is gone; and with him go these thoughts!
Now for the rebels which stand out in Ireland,
Expedient manage must be made, my liege,
Ere further leisure yield them further means   40
For their advantage and your Highness' loss.

King Richard

We will ourself in person to this war;
And, for our coffers, with too great a court
And liberal largess, are grown somewhat light,
We are enforc'd to farm our royal realm;   45
The revenue whereof shall furnish us
For our affairs in hand. If that come short,
Our substitutes at home shall have blank charters;
Whereto, when they shall know what men are rich,
They shall subscribe them for large sums of gold,   50
And send them after to supply our wants;
For we will make for Ireland presently.

[Enter BUSHY.]

Bushy, what news?

Bushy

Old John of Gaunt is grievous sick, my lord,
Suddenly taken; and hath sent post-haste   55

    To entreat your Majesty to visit him.
King Richard
    Where lies he?
Bushy
    At Ely House.
King Richard
    Now put it, God, in the physician's mind
60   To help him to his grave immediately!
    The lining of his coffers shall make coats
    To deck our soldiers for these Irish wars.
    Come, gentlemen, let's all go visit him.
    Pray God we may make haste, and come too late!
All
65   Amen.

[Exeunt.]

ACT TWO
Scene I

London. Ely House.

[Enter JOHN OF GAUNT, *sick, with the* DUKE OF YORK, *etc.]*

Gaunt

    Will the King come, that I may breathe my last

    In wholesome counsel to his unstaid youth?

York

    Vex not yourself, nor strive not with your breath;

    For all in vain comes counsel to his ear.

Gaunt

    O, but they say the tongues of dying men   5

    Enforce attention like deep harmony.

    Where words are scarce, they are seldom spent in
        vain;

    For they breathe truth that breathe their words in
        pain.

    He that no more must say is listen'd more

    Than they whom youth and ease have taught to
        glose;   10

    More are men's ends mark'd than their lives before.

    The setting sun, and music at the close,

    As the last taste of sweets, is sweetest last,

    Writ in remembrance more than things long past.

    Though Richard my life's counsel would not hear,   15

    My death's sad tale may yet undeaf his ear.

York

    No; it is stopp'd with other flattering sounds,

    As praises, of whose taste the wise are fond,

    Lascivious metres, to whose venom sound

    The open ear of youth doth always listen;   20

Report of fashions in proud Italy,
Whose manners still our tardy apish nation
Limps after in base imitation.
Where doth the world thrust forth a vanity –
25   So it be new, there's no respect how vile –
That is not quickly buzz'd into his ears?
Then all too late comes counsel to be heard
Where will doth mutiny with wit's regard.
Direct not him whose way himself will choose.
'Tis breath thou lack'st, and that breath wilt thou
30   lose.

Gaunt

Methinks I am a prophet new inspir'd,
And thus expiring do foretell of him:
His rash fierce blaze of riot cannot last,
For violent fires soon burn out themselves;
35   Small showers last long, but sudden storms are short;
He tires betimes that spurs too fast betimes;
With eager feeding food doth choke the feeder;
Light vanity, insatiate cormorant,
Consuming means, soon preys upon itself.
40   This royal throne of kings, this scept'red isle,
This earth of majesty, this seat of Mars,
This other Eden, demi-paradise,
This fortress built by Nature for herself
Against infection and the hand of war,
45   This happy breed of men, this little world,
This precious stone set in the silver sea,
Which serves it in the office of a wall,
Or as a moat defensive to a house,
Against the envy of less happier lands;
This blessed plot, this earth, this realm, this
50   England,
This nurse, this teeming womb of royal kings,
Fear'd by their breed, and famous by their birth,
Renowned for their deeds as far from home,
For Christian service and true chivalry,

As is the sepulchre in stubborn Jewry   55
Of the world's ransom, blessed Mary's Son;
This land of such dear souls, this dear dear land,
Dear for her reputation through the world,
Is now leas'd out – I die pronouncing it –
Like to a tenement or pelting farm.   60
England, bound in with the triumphant sea,
Whose rocky shore beats back the envious siege
Of wat'ry Neptune, is now bound in with shame,
With inky blots and rotten parchment bonds;
That England, that was wont to conquer others,   65
Hath made a shameful conquest of itself.
Ah, would the scandal vanish with my life,
How happy then were my ensuing death!

    [Enter KING *and* QUEEN, AUMERLE, BUSHY, GREEN,
        BAGOT, ROSS, *and* WILLOUGHBY.*]*

York
  The King is come; deal mildly with his youth,
  For young hot colts being rag'd do rage the more.   70
Queen
  How fares our noble uncle Lancaster?
King Richard
  What comfort, man? How is't with aged Gaunt?
Gaunt
  O, how that name befits my composition!
  Old Gaunt, indeed; and gaunt in being old.
  Within me grief hath kept a tedious fast;   75
  And who abstains from meat that is not gaunt?
  For sleeping England long time have I watch'd;
  Watching breeds leanness, leanness is all gaunt.
  The pleasure that some fathers feeds upon
  Is my strict fast – I mean my children's looks;   80
  And therein fasting, hast thou made me gaunt.
  Gaunt am I for the grave, gaunt as a grave,
  Whose hollow womb inherits nought but bones.

King Richard
> Can sick men play so nicely with their names?

Gaunt
85 > No, misery makes sport to mock itself:
> Since thou dost seek to kill my name in me,
> I mock my name, great king, to flatter thee.

King Richard
> Should dying men flatter with those that live?

Gaunt
> No, no; men living flatter those that die.

King Richard
90 > Thou, now a-dying, sayest thou flatterest me.

Gaunt
> O, no! thou diest, though I the sicker be.

King Richard
> I am in health, I breathe, and see thee ill.

Gaunt
> Now He that made me knows I see thee ill;
> Ill in myself to see, and in thee seeing ill.
95 > Thy death-bed is no lesser than thy land
> Wherein thou liest in reputation sick;
> And thou, too careless patient as thou art,
> Commit'st thy anointed body to the cure
> Of those physicians that first wounded thee:
100 > A thousand flatterers sit within thy crown,
> Whose compass is no bigger than thy head;
> And yet, incagéd in so small a verge,
> The waste is no whit lesser than thy land.
> O, had thy grandsire with a prophet's eye
105 > Seen how his son's son should destroy his sons,
> From forth thy reach he would have laid thy shame,
> Deposing thee before thou wert possess'd,
> Which art possess'd now to depose thyself.
> Why, cousin, wert thou regent of the world,
110 > It were a shame to let this land by lease;
> But for thy world enjoying but this land,
> Is it not more than shame to shame it so?

Landlord of England art thou now, not King.
Thy state of law is bondslave to the law;
And thou –
King Richard
           A lunatic lean-witted fool,   115
Presuming on an ague's privilege,
Darest with thy frozen admonition
Make pale our cheek, chasing the royal blood
With fury from his native residence.
Now by my seat's right royal majesty,   120
Wert thou not brother to great Edward's son,
This tongue that runs so roundly in thy head
Should run thy head from thy unreverent shoulders.
Gaunt
O, spare me not, my brother Edward's son,
For that I was his father Edward's son;   125
That blood already, like the pelican,
Hast thou tapp'd out, and drunkenly carous'd.
My brother Gloucester, plain well-meaning soul –
Whom fair befall in heaven 'mongst happy souls! –
May be a precedent and witness good   130
That thou respect'st not spilling Edward's blood.
Join with the present sickness that I have;
And thy unkindness be like crooked age,
To crop at once a too long withered flower.
Live in thy shame, but die not shame with thee!   135
These words hereafter thy tormentors be!
Convey me to my bed, then to my grave.
Love they to live that love and honour have.

[Exit, borne out by his Attendants.]

King Richard
And let them die that age and sullens have;
For both hast thou, and both become the grave.   140
York
I do beseech your Majesty impute his words
To wayward sickliness and age in him.

He loves you, on my life, and holds you dear
As Harry Duke of Hereford, were he here.

King Richard
145   Right, you say true: as Hereford's love, so his;
As theirs, so mine; and all be as it is.

[Enter NORTHUMBERLAND.*]*

Northumberland
My liege, old Gaunt commends him to your Majesty.
King Richard
What says he?
Northumberland
             Nay, nothing; all is said.
His tongue is now a stringless instrument;
150   Words, life, and all, old Lancaster hath spent.
York
Be York the next that must be bankrupt so!
Though death be poor, it ends a mortal woe.
King Richard
The ripest fruit first falls, and so doth he;
His time is spent, our pilgrimage must be.
155   So much for that. Now for our Irish wars.
We must supplant those rough rug-headed kerns,
Which live like venom where no venom else
But only they have privilege to live.
And for these great affairs do ask some charge,
160   Towards our assistance we do seize to us
The plate, coin, revenues, and moveables,
Whereof our uncle Gaunt did stand possess'd.
York
How long shall I be patient? Ah, how long
Shall tender duty make me suffer wrong?
165   Not Gloucester's death, nor Hereford's banishment,
Nor Gaunt's rebukes, nor England's private wrongs,
Nor the prevention of poor Bolingbroke
About his marriage, nor my own disgrace,
Have ever made me sour my patient cheek

Or bend one wrinkle on my sovereign's face.   170
I am the last of noble Edward's sons,
Of whom thy father, Prince of Wales, was first.
In war was never lion rag'd more fierce,
In peace was never gentle lamb more mild,
Than was that young and princely gentleman.   175
His face thou hast, for even so look'd he,
Accomplish'd with the number of thy hours;
But when he frown'd, it was against the French
And not against his friends. His noble hand
Did win what he did spend, and spent not that   180
Which his triumphant father's hand had won.
His hands were guilty of no kindred blood,
But bloody with the enemies of his kin.
O Richard! York is too far gone with grief,
Or else he never would compare between –   185

King Richard

   Why, uncle, what's the matter?

York

               O my liege,
Pardon me, if you please; if not, I, pleas'd
Not to be pardoned, am content withal.
Seek you to seize and gripe into your hands
The royalties and rights of banish'd Hereford?   190
Is not Gaunt dead? and doth not Hereford live?
Was not Gaunt just? and is not Harry true?
Did not the one deserve to have an heir?
Is not his heir a well-deserving son?
Take Hereford's rights away, and take from Time   195
His charters and his customary rights;
Let not to-morrow then ensue to-day;
Be not thyself – for how art thou a king
But by fair sequence and succession?
Now, afore God – God forbid I say true! –   200
If you do wrongfully seize Hereford's rights,
Call in the letters patents that he hath
By his attorneys-general to sue

His livery, and deny his off'red homage,
205 You pluck a thousand dangers on your head,
You lose a thousand well-disposed hearts,
And prick my tender patience to those thoughts
Which honour and allegiance cannot think.

King Richard
Think what you will, we seize into our hands
210 His plate, his goods, his money, and his lands.

York
I'll not be by the while. My liege, farewell.
What will ensue hereof there's none can tell;
But by bad courses may be understood
That their events can never fall out good.

[Exit.]

King Richard
215 Go, Bushy, to the Earl of Wiltshire straight;
Bid him repair to us to Ely House
To see this business. To-morrow next
We will for Ireland; and 'tis time, I trow.
And we create, in absence of ourself,
220 Our Uncle York Lord Governor of England;
For he is just, and always lov'd us well.
Come on, our queen; to-morrow must we part;
Be merry, for our time of stay is short.

[Flourish. Exeunt KING, QUEEN, BUSHY, AUMERLE,
GREEN, *and* BAGOT.*]*

Northumberland
Well, lords, the Duke of Lancaster is dead.
Ross
225 And living too; for now his son is Duke.
Willoughby
Barely in title, not in revenues.
Northumberland
Richly in both, if justice had her right.

Ross

    My heart is great; but it must break with silence,
    Ere't be disburdened with a liberal tongue.

Northumberland

    Nay, speak thy mind; and let him ne'er speak more   230
    That speaks thy words again to do thee harm!

Willoughby

    Tends that thou wouldst speak to the Duke of
       Hereford?
    If it be so, out with it boldly, man;
    Quick is mine ear to hear of good towards him.

Ross

    No good at all that I can do for him,   235
    Unless you call it good to pity him,
    Bereft and gelded of his patrimony.

Northumberland

    Now, afore God, 'tis shame such wrongs are borne
    In him, a royal prince, and many moe
    Of noble blood in this declining land.   240
    The King is not himself, but basely led
    By flatterers; and what they will inform,
    Merely in hate, 'gainst any of us all,
    That will the King severely prosecute
    'Gainst us, our lives, our children, and our hers.   245

Ross

    The commons hath he pill'd with grievous taxes;
    And quite lost their hearts; the nobles hath he fin'd
    For ancient quarrels and quite lost their hearts.

Willoughby

    And daily new exactions are devis'd,
    As blanks, benevolences, and I wot not what;   250
    But what, a God's name, doth become of this?

Northumberland

    Wars hath not wasted it, for warr'd he hath not,
    But basely yielded upon compromise
    That which his noble ancestors achiev'd with blows.
    More hath he spent in peace than they in wars.   255

Ross
    The Earl of Wiltshire hath the realm in farm.
Willoughby
    The King's grown bankrupt like a broken man.
Northumberland
    Reproach and dissolution hangeth over him.
Ross
    He hath not money for these Irish wars,
260   His burdenous taxations notwithstanding,
    But by the robbing of the banish'd Duke.
Northumberland
    His noble kinsman – most degenerate king!
    But, lords, we hear this fearful tempest sing,
    Yet seek no shelter to avoid the storm;
265   We see the wind sit sore upon our sails,
    And yet we strike not, but securely perish.
Ross
    We see the very wreck that we must suffer;
    And unavoided is the danger now
    For suffering so the causes of our wreck.
Northumberland
270   Not so; even through the hollow eyes of death
    I spy life peering; but I dare not say
    How near the tidings of our comfort is.
Willoughby
    Nay, let us share thy thoughts as thou dost ours.
Ross
    Be confident to speak, Northumberland.
275   We three are but thyself, and, speaking so,
    Thy words are but as thoughts; therefore be bold.
Northumberland
    Then thus: I have from Le Port Blanc, a bay
    In Brittany, receiv'd intelligence
    That Harry Duke of Hereford, Rainold Lord Cobham,
280   That late broke from the Duke of Exeter,
    His brother, Archbishop late of Canterbury,
    Sir Thomas Erpingham, Sir John Ramston,

Sir John Norbery, Sir Robert Waterton, and Francis
    Quoint –
All these, well furnish'd by the Duke of Britaine,
With eight tall ships, three thousand men of war,   285
Are making hither with all due expedience,
And shortly mean to touch our northern shore.
Perhaps they had ere this, but that they stay
The first departing of the King for Ireland.
If then we shall shake off our slavish yoke,   290
I'm out our drooping country's broken wing,
Redeem from broking pawn the blemish'd crown,
Wipe off the dust that hides our sceptre's gilt,
And make high majesty look like itself,
Away with me in post to Ravenspurgh;   295
But if you faint, as fearing to do so,
Stay and be secret, and myself will go.

Ross

To horse, to horse! Urge doubts to them that fear.

Willoughby

Hold out my horse, and I will first be there.

[Exeunt.]

Scene II

Windsor Castle.

[Enter QUEEN, BUSHY, *and* BAGOT.*]*

Bushy
    Madam, your Majesty is too much sad.
    You promis'd, when you parted with the King,
    To lay aside life-harming heaviness
    And entertain a cheerful disposition.

Queen
5   To please the King, I did; to please myself
    I cannot do it; yet I know no cause
    Why I should welcome such a guest as grief,
    Save bidding farewell to so sweet a guest
    As my sweet Richard. Yet again methinks
10   Some unborn sorrow, ripe in fortune's womb,
    Is coming towards me, and my inward soul
    With nothing trembles. At some thing it grieves
    More than with parting from my lord the King.

Bushy
    Each substance of a grief hath twenty shadows,
15   Which shows like grief itself, but is not so;
    For sorrow's eye, glazed with blinding tears,
    Divides one thing entire to many objects,
    Like perspectives which, rightly gaz'd upon,
    Show nothing but confusion – ey'd awry,
20   Distinguish form. So your sweet Majesty,
    Looking awry upon your lord's departure,
    Find shapes of grief more than himself to wail;
    Which, look'd on as it is, is nought but shadows
    Of what it is not. Then, thrice-gracious Queen,
    More than your lord's departure weep not – more is
25   not seen;
    Or if it be, 'tis with false sorrow's eye,
    Which for things true weeps things imaginary.

Queen

    It may be so; but yet my inward soul
    Persuades me it is otherwise. Howe'er it be,
    I cannot but be sad; so heavy sad   30
    As – though, on thinking, on no thought I think –
    Makes me with heavy nothing faint and shrink.

Bushy

    'Tis nothing but conceit, my gracious lady.

Queen

    'Tis nothing less: conceit is still deriv'd
    From some forefather grief; mine is not so,   35
    For nothing hath begot my something grief,
    Or something hath the nothing that I grieve;
    'Tis in reversion that I do possess –
    But what it is that is not yet known what,
    I cannot name; 'tis nameless woe, I wot.   40

[Enter GREEN.*]*

Green

    God save your Majesty! and well met, gentlemen.
    I hope the King is not yet shipp'd for Ireland.

Queen

    Why hopest thou so? 'Tis better hope he is;
    For his designs crave haste, his haste good hope.
    Then wherefore dost thou hope he is not shipp'd?   45

Green

    That he, our hope, might have retir'd his power
    And driven into despair an enemy'd hope
    Who strongly hath set footing in this land.
    The banish'd Bolingbroke repeals himself,
    And with uplifted arms is safe arriv'd   50
    At Ravenspurgh.

Queen

                  Now God in heaven forbid!

Green

    Ah, madam, 'tis too true; and that is worse,
    The Lord Northumberland, his son young Henry Percy,

The Lords of Ross, Beaumond, and Willoughby,
55   With all their powerful friends, are fled to him.

Bushy

Why have you not proclaim'd Northumberland
And all the rest revolted faction traitors?

Green

We have; whereupon the Earl of Worcester
Hath broken his staff, resign'd his stewardship,
60   And all the household servants fled with him
To Bolingbroke.

Queen

So, Green, thou art the midwife to my woe,
And Bolingbroke my sorrow's dismal heir.
Now hath my soul brought forth her prodigy;
65   And I, a gasping new-deliver'd mother,
Have woe to woe, sorrow to sorrow join'd.

Bushy

Despair not, madam.

Queen

                Who shall hinder me?
I will despair, and be at enmity
With cozening hope – he is a flatterer,
70   A parasite, a keeper-back of death,
Who gently would dissolve the bands of life,
Which false hope lingers in extremity.

[Enter YORK.]

Green

Here comes the Duke of York.

Queen

With signs of war about his aged neck.
75   O, full of careful business are his looks!
Uncle, for God's sake, speak comfortable words.

York

Should I do so, I should belie my thoughts.
Comfort's in heaven; and we are on the earth,
Where nothing lives but crosses, cares, and grief.

Your husband, he is gone to save far off,   80
Whilst others come to make him lose at home.
Here am I left to underprop his land,
Who, weak with age, cannot support myself.
Now comes the sick hour that his surfeit made;
Now shall he try his friends that flatter'd him.   85

[Enter a Servant.]

Servant
My lord, your son was gone before I came.
York
He was – why so go all which way it will!
The nobles they are fled, the commons they are cold
And will, I fear, revolt on Hereford's side.
Sirrah, get thee to Plashy, to my sister Gloucester;   90
Bid her send me presently a thousand pound.
Hold, take my ring.
Servant
My lord, I had forgot to tell your lordship,
To-day, as I came by, I called there –
But I shall grieve you to report the rest.   95
York
What is't, knave?
Servant
An hour before I came, the Duchess died.
York
God for his mercy! what a tide of woes
Comes rushing on this woeful land at once!
I know not what to do. I would to God,   100
So my untruth had not provok'd him to it,
The King had cut off my head with my brother's.
What, are there no posts dispatch'd for Ireland?
How shall we do for money for these wars?
Come, sister – cousin, I would say – pray, pardon
   me.   105
Go, fellow, get thee home, provide some carts,
And bring away the armour that is there.

[Exit Servant.]

Gentlemen, will you go muster men?
If I know how or which way to order these affairs
110   Thus disorderly thrust into my hands,
Never believe me. Both are my kinsmen.
T'one is my sovereign, whom both my oath
And duty bids defend; t'other again
Is my kinsman, whom the King hath wrong'd,
115   Whom conscience and my kindred bids to right.
Well, somewhat we must do. – Come, cousin,
I'll dispose of you. Gentlemen, go muster up your
    men,
And meet me presently at Berkeley.
I should to Plashy too,
120   But time will not permit. All is uneven,
And everything is left at six and seven.

[Exeunt YORK and QUEEN.]

Bushy
The wind sits fair for news to go to Ireland.
But none returns. For us to levy power
Proportionable to the enemy
125   Is all unpossible.
Green
Besides, our nearness to the King in love
Is near the hate of those love not the King.
Bagot
And that is the wavering commons; for their love
Lies in their purses; and whoso empties them,
130   By so much fills their hearts with deadly hate.
Bushy
Wherein the King stands generally condemn'd.
Bagot
If judgment lie in them, then so do we,
Because we ever have been near the King.
Green
Well, I will for refuge straight to Bristow Castle.

The Earl of Wiltshire is already there. 135

Bushy

Thither will I with you; for little office
Will the hateful commons perform for us, Except
like curs to tear us all to pieces.
Will you go along with us?

Bagot

No; I will to Ireland to his Majesty.
Farewell. If heart's presages be not vain, 140
We three here part that ne'er shall meet again.

Bushy

That's as York thrives to beat back Bolingbroke.

Green

Alas, poor Duke! the task he undertakes
Is numb'ring sands and drinking oceans dry.
Where one on his side fights, thousands will fly. 145
Farewell at once – for once, for all, and ever.

Bushy

Well, we may meet again.

Bagot

I fear me, never.

[Exeunt.]

Scene III

Gloucestershire.

[Enter BOLINGBROKE and NORTHUMBERLAND, with Forces.]

Bolingbroke
How far is it, my lord, to Berkeley now?
Northumberland
Believe me, noble lord,
I am a stranger here in Gloucestershire.
These high wild hills and rough uneven ways
5   Draws out our miles, and makes them wearisome;
And yet your fair discourse hath been as sugar,
Making the hard way sweet and delectable.
But I bethink me what a weary way
From Ravenspurgh to Cotswold will be found
10   In Ross and Willoughby, wanting your company,
Which, I protest, hath very much beguil'd
The tediousness and process of my travel.
But theirs is sweet'ned with the hope to have
The present benefit which I possess;
15   And hope to joy is little less in joy
Than hope enjoy'd. By this the weary lords
Shall make their way seem short, as mine hath done
By sight of what I have, your noble company.
Bolingbroke
Of much less value is my company
20   Than your good words. But who comes here?

[Enter HARRY PERCY.]

Northumberland
It is my son, young Harry Percy,
Sent from my brother Worcester, whencesoever.
Harry, how fares your uncle?
Percy
I had thought, my lord, to have learn'd his health of
you.

Northumberland
Why, is he not with the Queen?   25
Percy
No, my good lord; he hath forsook the court,
Broken his staff of office, and dispers'd
The household of the King.
Northumberland
                        What was his reason?
He was not so resolv'd when last we spake together.
Percy
Because your lordship was proclaimed traitor.   30
But he, my lord, is gone to Ravenspurgh,
To offer service to the Duke of Hereford;
And sent me over by Berkeley, to discover
What power the Duke of York had levied there;
Then with directions to repair to Ravenspurgh.   35
Northumberland
Have you forgot the Duke of Hereford, boy?
Percy
No, my good lord; for that is not forgot
Which ne'er I did remember; to my knowledge,
I never in my life did look on him.
Northumberland
Then learn to know him now; this is the Duke.   40
Percy
My gracious lord, I tender you my service,
Such as it is, being tender, raw, and young;
Which elder days shall ripen, and confirm
To more approved service and desert.
Bolingbroke
I thank thee, gentle Percy; and be sure   45
I count myself in nothing else so happy
As in a soul rememb'ring my good friends;
And as my fortune ripens with thy love,
It shall be still thy true love's recompense.
My heart this covenant makes, my hand thus seals
     it.   50

Northumberland
> How far is it to Berkeley? And what stir
> Keeps good old York there with his men of war?

Percy
> There stands the castle, by yon tuft of trees,
> Mann'd with three hundred men, as I have heard;
> And in it are the Lords of York, Berkeley, and
55 > Seymour –
> None else of name and noble estimate.

[Enter ROSS and WILLOUGHBY.]

Northumberland
> Here come the Lords of Ross and Willoughby,
> Bloody with spurring, fiery-red with haste.

Bolingbroke
> Welcome, my lords. I wot your love pursues
60 > A banish'd traitor. All my treasury
> Is yet but unfelt thanks, which, more enrich'd,
> Shall be your love and labour's recompense.

Ross
> Your presence makes us rich, most noble lord.

Willoughby
> And far surmounts our labour to attain it.

Bolingbroke
65 > Evermore thanks, the exchequer of the poor;
> Which, till my infant fortune comes to years,
> Stands for my bounty. But who comes here?

[Enter BERKELEY.]

Northumberland
> It is my Lord of Berkeley, as I guess.

Berkeley
> My Lord of Hereford, my message is to you.

Bolingbroke
70 > My lord, my answer is – 'to Lancaster';
> And I am come to seek that name in England;
> And I must find that title in your tongue

Before I make reply to aught you say.
Berkeley
Mistake me not, my lord; 'tis not my meaning
To raze one title of your honour out.   75
To you, my lord, I come – what lord you will –
From the most gracious regent of this land,
The Duke of York, to know what pricks you on
To take advantage of the absent time,
And fright our native peace with self-borne arms.   80

[Enter YORK, attended.]

Bolingbroke
I shall not need transport my words by you;
Here comes his Grace in person. My noble uncle!
   [Kneels.]
York
Show me thy humble heart, and not thy knee,
Whose duty is deceivable and false.
Bolingbroke
My gracious uncle! –   85
York
Tut, tut!
Grace me no grace, nor uncle me no uncle.
I am no traitor's uncle; and that word 'grace'
In an ungracious mouth is but profane.
Why have those banish'd and forbidden legs   90
Dar'd once to touch a dust of England's ground?
But then more 'why?' – why have they dar'd to
      march
So many miles upon her peaceful bosom,
Frighting her pale-fac'd villages with war
And ostentation of despised arms?   95
Com'st thou because the anointed King is hence?
Why, foolish boy, the King is left behind,
And in my loyal bosom lies his power.
Were I but now lord of such hot youth
As when brave Gaunt, thy father, and myself   100

Rescued the Black Prince, that young Mars of men,
From forth the ranks of many thousand French,
O, then how quickly should this arm of mine,
Now prisoner to the palsy, chastise thee
105 And minister correction to thy fault!
Bolingbroke
My gracious uncle, let me know my fault;
On what condition stands it and wherein?
York
Even in condition of the worst degree –
In gross rebellion and detested treason.
110 Thou art a banish'd man, and here art come
Before the expiration of thy time,
In braving arms against thy sovereign.
Bolingbroke
As I was banish'd, I was banish'd Hereford;
But as I come, I come for Lancaster.
115 And, noble uncle, I beseech your Grace
Look on my wrongs with an indifferent eye.
You are my father, for methinks in you
I see old Gaunt alive. O, then, my father,
Will you permit that I shall stand condemn'd
120 A wandering vagabond; my rights and royalties
Pluck'd from my arms perforce, and given away
To upstart unthrifts? Wherefore was I born?
If that my cousin king be King in England,
It must be granted I am Duke of Lancaster.
125 You have a son, Aumerle, my noble cousin;
Had you first died, and he been thus trod down,
He should have found his uncle Gaunt a father
To rouse his wrongs and chase them to the bay.
I am denied to sue my livery here,
130 And yet my letters patents give me leave.
My father's goods are all distrain'd and sold;
And these and all are all amiss employ'd.
What would you have me do? I am a subject,
And I challenge law – attorneys are denied me;

And therefore personally I lay my claim 135
To my inheritance of free descent.

Northumberland
The noble Duke hath been too much abused.

Ross
It stands your Grace upon to do him right.

Willoughby
Base men by his endowments are made great.

York
My lords of England, let me tell you this: 140
I have had feeling of my cousin's wrongs,
And labour'd all I could to do him right;
But in this kind to come, in braving arms,
Be his own carver and cut out his way,
To find out right with wrong – it may not be; 145
And you that do abet him in this kind
Cherish rebellion, and are rebels all.

Northumberland
The noble Duke hath sworn his coming is
But for his own; and for the right of that
We all have strongly sworn to give him aid; 150
And let him never see joy that breaks that oath!

York
Well, well, I see the issue of these arms.
I cannot mend it, I must needs confess,
Because my power is weak and all ill left;
But if I could, by Him that gave me life, 155
I would attach you all and make you stoop
Unto the sovereign mercy of the King;
But since I cannot, be it known unto you
I do remain as neuter. So, fare you well;
Unless you please to enter in the castle, 160
And there repose you for this night.

Bolingbroke
An offer, uncle, that we will accept.
But we must win your Grace to go with us
To Bristow Castle, which they say is held

165 By Bushy, Bagot, and their complices,
  The caterpillars of the commonwealth,
  Which I have sworn to weed and pluck away.

York

  It may be I will go with you; but yet I'll pause,
  For I am loath to break our country's laws.

170 Nor friends nor foes, to me welcome you are.
  Things past redress are now with me past care.

[Exeunt.]

Scene IV

A camp in Wales.

[Enter EARL OF SALISBURY *and a Welsh Captain.]*

Captain

My Lord of Salisbury, we have stay'd ten days
And hardly kept our countrymen together,
And yet we hear no tidings from the King;
Therefore we will disperse ourselves. Farewell.

Salisbury

Stay yet another day, thou trusty Welshman;   5
The king reposeth all his confidence in thee.

Captain

'Tis thought the King is dead; we will not stay.
The bay trees in our country are all wither'd,
And meteors fright the fixed stars of heaven;
The pale-fac'd moon looks bloody on the earth,   10
And lean-look'd prophets whisper fearful change;
Rich men look sad, and ruffians dance and leap –
The one in fear to lose what they enjoy,
The other to enjoy by rage and war.
These signs forerun the death or fall of kings.   15
Farewell. Our countrymen are gone and fled,
As well assur'd Richard their King is dead.

[Exit.]

Salisbury

Ah, Richard, with the eyes of heavy mind,
I see thy glory like a shooting star
Fall to the base earth from the firmament!   20
The sun sets weeping in the lowly west,
Witnessing storms to come, woe, and unrest;
Thy friends are fled, to wait upon thy foes;
And crossly to thy good all fortune goes. *[Exit.]*

ACT THREE

Scene I

Bolingbroke's camp at Bristol.

[*Enter* BOLINGBROKE, YORK, NORTHUMBERLAND,
PERCY, ROSS, WILLOUGHBY, *with* BUSHY *and* GREEN,
prisoners.]

Bolingbroke
　　　Bring forth these men.
　　　Bushy and Green, I will not vex your souls –
　　　Since presently your souls must part your bodies –
　　　With too much urging your pernicious lives,
5　　For 'twere no charity; yet, to wash your blood
　　　From off my hands, here in the view of men
　　　I will unfold some causes of your deaths:
　　　You have misled a prince, a royal king,
　　　A happy gentleman in blood and lineaments,
10　By you unhappied and disfigured clean;
　　　You have in manner with your sinful hours
　　　Made a divorce betwixt his queen and him;
　　　Broke the possession of a royal bed,
　　　And stain'd the beauty of a fair queen's cheeks
　　　With tears drawn from her eyes by your foul
15　　　wrongs;
　　　Myself – a prince by fortune of my birth,
　　　Near to the King in blood, and near in love
　　　Till you did make him misinterpret me –
　　　Have stoop'd my neck under your injuries
20　And sigh'd my English breath in foreign clouds,
　　　Eating the bitter bread of banishment,
　　　Whilst you have fed upon my signories,
　　　Dispark'd my parks and fell'd my forest woods,
　　　From my own windows torn my household coat,

Raz'd out my imprese, leaving me no sign   25
Save men's opinions and my living blood
To show the world I am a gentleman.
This and much more, much more than twice all
    this,
Condemns you to the death. See them delivered
    over
To execution and the hand of death.   30

Bushy
More welcome is the stroke of death to me
Than Bolingbroke to England. Lords, farewell.

Green
My comfort is that heaven will take our souls,
And plague injustice with the pains of hell.

Bolingbroke
My Lord Northumberland, see them dispatch'd.   35

[Exeunt NORTHUMBERLAND, *and others, with the
prisoners.]*

Uncle, you say the Queen is at your house;
For God's sake, fairly let her be entreated.
Tell her I send to her my kind commends;
Take special care my greetings be delivered.

York
A gentleman of mine I have dispatch'd   40
With letters of your love to her at large.

Bolingbroke
Thanks, gentle uncle. Come, lords, away,
To fight with Glendower and his complices.
A while to work, and after holiday.

[Exeunt.]

Scene II

The coast of Wales. A castle in view.

[Drums. Flourish and colours. Enter the KING, *the* BISHOP OF CARLISLE, AUMERLE *and Soldiers.]*

King Richard
    Barkloughly Castle call they this at hand?
Aumerle
    Yea, my lord. How brooks your Grace the air
    After your late tossing on the breaking seas?
King Richard
    Needs must I like it well. I weep for joy
5   To stand upon my kingdom once again.
    Dear earth, I do salute thee with my hand,
    Though rebels wound thee with their horses' hoofs.
    As a long-parted mother with her child
    Plays fondly with her tears and smiles in meeting,
10 So weeping-smiling greet I thee, my earth,
    And do thee favours with my royal hands.
    Feed not thy sovereign's foe, my gentle earth,
    Nor with thy sweets comfort his ravenous sense;
    But let thy spiders, that suck up thy venom,
15 And heavy-gaited toads, lie in their way,
    Doing annoyance to the treacherous feet
    Which with usurping steps do trample thee;
    Yield stinging nettles to mine enemies;
    And when they from thy bosom pluck a flower,
20 Guard it, I pray thee, with a lurking adder,
    Whose double tongue may with a mortal touch
    Throw death upon thy sovereign's enemies.
    Mock not my senseless conjuration, lords.
    This earth shall have a feeling, and these stones
25 Prove armed soldiers, ere her native King
    Shall falter under foul rebellion's arms.
Carlisle
    Fear not, my lord; that Power that made you king
    Hath power to keep you king in spite of all.

The means that heaven yields must be embrac'd
And not neglected; else, if heaven would,   30
And we will not, heaven's offer we refuse,
The proffered means of succour and redress.

Aumerle

He means, my lord, that we are too remiss;
Whilst Bolingbroke, through our security,
Grows strong and great in substance and in power.   35

King Richard

Discomfortable cousin! know'st thou not
That when the searching eye of heaven is hid,
Behind the globe, that lights the lower world,
Then thieves and robbers range abroad unseen
In murders and in outrage boldly here;   40
But when from under this terrestrial ball
He fires the proud tops of the eastern pines
And darts his light through every guilty hole,
Then murders, treasons, and detested sins,
The cloak of night being pluck'd from off their backs, 45
Stand bare and naked, trembling at themselves?
So when this thief, this traitor, Bolingbroke,
Who all this while hath revell'd in the night,
Whilst we were wand'ring with the Antipodes,
Shall see us rising in our throne, the east,   50
His treasons will sit blushing in his face,
Not able to endure the sight of day,
But self-affrighted tremble at his sin.
Not all the water in the rough rude sea
Can wash the balm off from an anointed king;   55
The breath of worldly men cannot despose
The deputy elected by the Lord.
For every man that Bolingbroke hath press'd
To lift shrewd steel against our golden crown,
God for his Richard hath in heavenly pay   60
A glorious angel. Then, if angels fight,
Weak men must fall; for heaven still guards the right.

[Enter SALISBURY.*]*

Welcome, my lord. How far off lies your power?
Salisbury
    Nor near nor father off, my gracious lord,
65   Than this weak arm. Discomfort guides my tongue,
    And bids me speak of nothing but despair.
    One day too late, I fear me, noble lord,
    Hath clouded all thy happy days on earth.
    O, call back yesterday, bid time return,
70   And thou shalt have twelve thousand fighting men!
    To-day, to-day, unhappy day, too late,
    O'erthrows thy joys, friends, fortune, and thy state;
    For all the Welshmen, hearing thou wert dead,
    Are gone to Bolingbroke, dispers'd, and fled.
Aumerle
75   Comfort, my liege, why looks your Grace so pale?
King Richard
    But now the blood of twenty thousand men
    Did triumph in my face, and they are fled;
    And, till so much blood thither come again,
    Have I not reason to look pale and dead?
80   All souls that will be safe, fly from my side;
    For time hath set a blot upon my pride.
Aumerle
    Comfort, my liege; remember who you are.
King Richard
    I had forgot myself; am I not King?
    Awake, thou coward majesty! thou sleepest.
85   Is not the King's name twenty thousand names?
    Arm, arm, my name! a puny subject strikes
    At thy great glory. Look not to the ground,
    Ye favourites of a king; are we not high?
    High be our thoughts. I know my uncle York
    Hath power enough to serve our turn. But who
90   comes here?

[Enter SCROOP.*]*

Scroop
    More health and happiness betide my liege

Than can my care-tun'd tongue deliver him.

King Richard

Mine ear is open and my heart prepar'd.
The worst is worldly loss thou canst unfold.
Say, is my kingdom lost? Why, 'twas my care;   95
And what loss is it to be rid of care?
Strives Bolingbroke to be as great as we?
Greater he shall not be; if he serve God,
We'll serve him too, and be his fellow so.
Revolt our subjects? That we cannot mend;   100
They break their faith to God as well as us.
Cry woe, destruction, ruin, and decay –
The worst is death, and death will have his day.

Scroop

Glad am I that your Highness is so arm'd
To bear the tidings of calamity.   105
Like an unseasonable stormy day
Which makes the silver rivers drown their shores,
As if the world were all dissolv'd to tears,
So high above his limits swells the rage
Of Bolingbroke, covering your fearful land   110
With hard bright steel and hearts harder than steel.
White-beards have arm'd their thin and hairless
    scalps
Against thy majesty; boys, with women's voices,
Strive to speak big, and clap their female joints
In stiff unwieldly arms against thy crown;   115
Thy very beadsmen learn to bend their bows
Of double-fatal yew against thy state;
Yea, distaff-women manage rusty bills
Against thy seat: both young and old rebel,
And all goes worse than I have power to tell.   120

King Richard

Too well, too well thou tell'st a tale so ill.
Where is the Earl of Wiltshire? Where is Bagot?
What is become of Bushy? Where is Green?
That they have let the dangerous enemy
Measure our confines with such peaceful steps?   125

If we prevail, their heads shall pay for it.
I warrant they have made peace with Bolingbroke.

Scroop

Peace have they made with him indeed, my lord.

King Richard

O villains, vipers, damn'd without redemption!
130 Dogs, easily won to fawn on any man!
Snakes, in my heart-blood warm'd, that sting my
    heart!
Three Judases, each one thrice worse than Judas!
Would they make peace? Terrible hell make war
Upon their spotted souls for this offence!

Scroop

135 Sweet love, I see, changing his property,
Turns to the sourest and most deadly hate.
Again uncurse their souls; their peace is made
With heads, and not with hands; those whom you
    curse
Have felt the worst of death's destroying wound
140 And lie full low, grav'd in the hollow ground.

Aumerle

Is Bushy, Green, and the Earl of Wiltshire dead?

Scroop

Ay, all of them at Bristow lost their heads.

Aumerle

Where is the Duke my father with his power?

King Richard

No matter where – of comfort no man speak.
145 Let's talk of graves, of worms, and epitaphs;
Make dust our paper, and with rainy eyes
Write sorrow on the bosom of the earth.
Let's choose executors and talk of wills;
And yet not so – for what can we bequeath
150 Save our deposed bodies to the ground?
Our lands, our lives, and all, are Bolingbroke's.
And nothing can we call our own but death
And that small model of the barren earth
Which serves as paste and cover to our bones.

For God's sake let us sit upon the ground 155
And tell sad stories of the death of kings:
How some have been depos'd, some slain in war,
Some haunted by the ghosts they have depos'd,
Some poison'd by their wives, some sleeping kill'd,
All murder'd – for within the hollow crown 160
That rounds the mortal temples of a king
Keeps Death his court; and there the antic sits,
Scoffing his state and grinning at his pomp;
Allowing him a breath, a little scene,
To monarchize, be fear'd, and kill with looks; 165
Infusing him with self and vain conceit,
As if this flesh which walls about our life
Were brass impregnable; and, humour'd thus,
Comes at the last, and with a little pin
Bores through his castle wall, and farewell, king! 170
Cover your heads, and mock not flesh and blood
With solemn reverence; throw away respect,
Tradition, form, and ceremonious duty;
For you have but mistook me all this while.
I live with bread like you, feel want, 175
Taste grief, need friends; subjected thus,
How can you say to me I am a king?

Carlisle

My lord, wise men ne'er sit and wail their woes,
But presently prevent the ways to wail.
To fear the foe, since fear oppresseth strength, 180
Gives, in your weakness, strength unto your foe,
And so your follies fight against yourself.
Fear and be slain – no worse can come to fight;
And fight and die is death destroying death,
Where fearing dying pays death servile breath. 185

Aumerle

My father hath a power; inquire of him,
And learn to make a body of a limb.

King Richard

Thou chid'st me well. Proud Bolingbroke, I come
To change blows with thee for our day of doom.

190   This ague fit of fear is over-blown;
       An easy task it is to win our own.
       Say, Scroop, where lies our uncle with his power?
       Speak sweetly, man, although thy looks be sour.

Scroop
       Men judge by the complexion of the sky
195   The state and inclination of the day;
       So may you by my dull and heavy eye,
       My tongue hath but a heavier tale to say.
       I play the torturer, by small and small
       To lengthen out the worst that must be spoken:
200   Your uncle York is join'd with Bolingbroke;
       And all your northern castles yielded up,
       And all your southern gentlemen in arms
       Upon his party.

King Richard
                  Thou hast said enough.
       [To Aumerle] Beshrew thee, cousin, which didst lead
          me forth
205   Of that sweet way I was in to despair!
       What say you now? What comfort have we now?
       By heaven, I'll hate him everlastingly
       That bids me be of comfort any more.
       Go to Flint Castle; there I'll pine away;
210   A king, woe's slave, shall kingly woe obey.
       That power I have, discharge; and let them go
       To ear the land that hath some hope to grow,
       For I have none. Let no man speak again
       To alter this, for counsel is but vain.

Aumerle
       My liege, one word.

King Richard
215   He does me double wrong
       That wounds me with the flatteries of his tongue.
       Discharge my followers; let them hence away,
       From Richard's night to Bolingbroke's fair day.

[Exeunt.]

Scene III

Wales. Before Flint Castle.

[Enter, with drum and colours, BOLINGBROKE, YORK,
NORTHUMBERLAND, *and Forces.]*

Bolingbroke
So that by this intelligence we learn
The Welshmen are dispers'd; and Salisbury
Is gone to meet the King, who lately landed
With some few private friends upon this coast.

Northumberland
The news is very fair and good, my lord.   5
Richard not far from hence hath hid his head.

York
It would beseem the Lord Northumberland
To say 'King Richard'. Alack the heavy day
When such a sacred king should hide his head!

Northumberland
Your Grace mistakes; only to be brief,   10
Left I his title out.

York
    The time hath been,
Would you have been so brief with him, he would
Have been so brief with you to shorten you,
For taking so the head, your whole head's length.

Bolingbroke
Mistake not, uncle, further than you should.   15

York
Take not, good cousin, further than you should,
Lest you mistake. The heavens are over our heads.

Bolingbroke
I know it, uncle; and oppose not myself
Against their will. But who comes here?

[Enter PERCY.*]*

Welcome, Harry. What, will not this castle yield?   20

Percy
The castle royally is mann'd, my lord,
Against thy entrance.
Bolingbroke
Royally!
Why, it contains no king?
Percy
                      Yes, my good lord,

25   It doth contain a king; King Richard lies
      Within the limits of yon lime and stone;
      And with him are the Lord Aumerle, Lord Salisbury,
      Sir Stephen Scroop, besides a clergyman
      Of holy reverence; who, I cannot learn.
Northumberland
30   O, belike it is the Bishop of Carlisle.
Bolingbroke
      [To NORTHUMBERLAND*]* Noble lord,
      Go to the rude ribs of that ancient castle;
      Through brazen trumpet send the breath of parley
      Into his ruin'd ears, and thus deliver:
35   Henry Bolingbroke
      On both his knees doth kiss King Richard's hand,
      And sends allegiance and true faith of heart
      To his most royal person; hither come
      Even at his feet to lay my arms and power,
40   Provided that my banishment repeal'd
      And lands restor'd again be freely granted;
      If not, I'll use the advantage of my power
      And lay the summer's dust with showers of blood
      Rain'd from the wounds of slaughtered Englishmen;
      The which how far off from the mind of
45   Bolingbroke
      It is such crimson tempest should bedrench
      The fresh green lap of fair King Richard's land,
      My stooping duty tenderly shall show.
      Go, signify as much, while here we march
50   Upon the grassy carpet of this plain.

[NORTHUMBERLAND advances to the Castle, with a trumpet.]

Let's march without the noise of threat'ning drum,
That from this castle's tottered battlements
Our fair appointments may be well perus'd.
Methinks King Richard and myself should meet
With no less terror than the elements   55
Of fire and water, when their thund'ring shock
At meeting tears the cloudy cheeks of heaven.
Be he the fire, I'll be the yielding water;
The rage be his, whilst on the earth I rain
My waters – on the earth, and not on him.   60
March on, and mark King Richard how he looks.

[Parle without, and answer within; then a flourish.]

*[Enter on the walls, the KING, the BISHOP OF CARLISLE,
AUMERLE, SCROOP and SALISBURY.]*

See, see, King Richard doth himself appear,
As doth the blushing discontented sun
From out the fiery portal of the east,
When he perceives the envious clouds are bent   65
To dim his glory and to stain the track
Of his bright passage to the occident.
York
Yet looks he like a king. Behold, his eye,
As bright as is the eagle's, lightens forth
Controlling majesty. Alack, alack, for woe,   75
That any harm should stain so fair a show!
King Richard
[To NORTHUMBERLAND] We are amaz'd; and thus
      long have we stood
To watch the fearful bending of thy knee,
Because we thought ourself thy lawful king;
And if we be, how dare thy joints forget   75
To pay their awful duty to our presence?
If we be not, show us the hand of God

That hath dismiss'd us from our stewardship;
For well we know no hand of blood and bone
80   Can gripe the sacred handle of our sceptre,
Unless he do profane, steal, or usurp.
And though you think that all, as you have done,
Have torn their souls by turning them from us,
And we are barren and bereft of friends,
85   Yet know – my master, God omnipotent,
Is mustering in his clouds on our behalf
Armies of pestilence; and they shall strike
Your children yet unborn and unbegot,
That lift your vassal hands against my head
90   And threat the glory of my precious crown.
Tell Bolingbroke, for yon methinks he stands,
That every stride he makes upon my land
Is dangerous treason; he is come to open
The purple testament of bleeding war;
95   But ere the crown he looks for live in peace,
Ten thousand bloody crowns of mothers' sons
Shall ill become the flower of England's face,
Change the complexion of her maid-pale peace
To scarlet indignation, and bedew
100   Her pastures' grass with faithful English blood.
   Northumberland
The King of Heaven forbid our lord the King
Should so with civil and uncivil arms
Be rush'd upon! Thy thrice noble cousin,
Harry Bolingbroke, doth humbly kiss thy hand;
105   And by the honourable tomb he swears
That stands upon your royal grandsire's bones,
And by the royalties of both your bloods,
Currents that spring from one most gracious head,
And by the buried hand of warlike Gaunt,
110   And by the worth and honour of himself,
Comprising all that may be sworn or said,
His coming hither hath no further scope
Than for his lineal royalties, and to beg

Enfranchisement immediate on his knees;
Which on thy royal party granted once,   115
His glittering arms he will commend to rust,
His barbed steeds to stables, and his heart
To faithful service of your Majesty.
This swears he, as he is a prince, is just;
And as I am a gentleman I credit him.   120

King Richard
Northumberland, say thus the King returns:
His noble cousin is right welcome hither;
And all the number of his fair demands
Shall be accomplish'd without contradiction.
With all the gracious utterance thou hast   125
Speak to his gentle hearing kind commends.
[To AUMERLE*]* We do debase ourselves, cousin, do we
    not,
To look so poorly and to speak so fair?
Shall we call back Northumberland, and send
Defiance to the traitor, and so die?   130

Aumberle
No, good my lord; let's fight with gentle words
Till time lend friends, and friends their helpful
    swords.

King Richard
O God, O God! that e'er this tongue of mine
That laid the sentence of dread banishment
On yon proud man should take it off again   135
With words of sooth! O that I were as great
As is my grief, or lesser than my name!
Or that I could forget what I have been!
Or not remember what I must be now!
Swell'st thou, proud heart? I'll give thee scope to
    beat,   140
Since foes have scope to beat both thee and me.

Aumerle
Northumberland comes back from Bolingbroke.

King Richard
What must the King do now?
Must he submit?
145 The King shall do it. Must he be depos'd?
The King shall be contented. Must he lose
The name of king? A God's name, let it go.
I'll give my jewels for a set of beads,
My gorgeous palace for a hermitage,
150 My gay apparel for an almsman's gown,
My figur'd goblets for a dish of wood,
My sceptre for a palmer's walking staff,
My subjects for a pair of carved saints,
And my large kingdom for a little grave,
155 A little little grave, an obscure grave –
Or I'll be buried in the king's high way,
Some way of common trade, where subjects' feet
May hourly trample on their sovereign's head;
For on my heart they tread now whilst I live,
160 And buried once, why not upon my head?
Aumerle, thou weep'st, my tender-hearted cousin!
We'll make foul weather with despised tears;
Our sighs and they shall lodge the summer corn
And make a dearth in this revolting land.
165 Or shall we play the wantons with our woes
And make some pretty match with shedding tears?
As thus: to drop them still upon one place
Till they have fretted us a pair of graves
Within the earth; and, therein laid – there lies
170 Two kinsmen digg'd their graves with weeping eyes.
Would not this ill do well? Well, well, I see
I talk but idly, and you laugh at me.
Most mighty prince, my Lord Northumberland,
What says King Bolingbroke? Will his Majesty
175 Give Richard leave to live till Richard die?
You make a leg, and Bolingbroke says ay.
Northumberland
My lord, in the base court he doth attend

To speak with you; may it please you to come
    down?
King Richard
    Down, down I come, like glist'ring Phaethon,
    Wanting the manage of unruly jades. 180
    In the base court? Base court, where kings grow
        base,
    To come at traitors' calls, and do them grace.
    In the base court? Come down? Down, court! down,
        king!
    For night-owls shriek where mounting larks should
        sing. *[Exeunt from above.]*
Bolingbroke
    What says his Majesty?
Northumberland
                  Sorrow and grief of heart 185
    Makes him speak fondly, like a frantic man;
    Yet he is come.

[Enter the KING, *and his Attendants, below.]*

Bolingbroke
    Stand all apart,
    And show fair duty to his Majesty.

[He kneels down.]

    My gracious lord – 190
King Richard
    Fair cousin, you debase your princely knee
    To make the base earth proud with kissing it.
    Me rather had my heart might feel your love
    Than my unpleas'd eye see your courtesy.
    Up, cousin, up; your heart is up, I know, 195
    [Touching his own head] Thus high at least, although
        your knee be low.
Bolingbroke
    My gracious lord, I come but for mine own.

King Richard
Your own is yours, and I am yours, and all.
Bolingbroke
So far be mine, my most redoubted lord,
200 As my true service shall deserve your love.
King Richard
Well you deserve. They well deserve to have
That know the strong'st and surest way to get.
Uncle, give me your hands; nay, dry your eyes:
Tears show their love, but want their remedies.
205 Cousin, I am too young to be your father,
Though you are old enough to be my heir.
What you will have, I'll give, and willing too;
For do we must what force will have us do.
Set on towards London. Cousin, is it so?
Bolingbroke
Yea, my good lord.
King Richard
205   Then I must not say no.

[Flourish. Exeunt.]

Scene IV

The Duke of York's garden.

[Enter the QUEEN and two Ladies.]

Queen
　What sport shall we devise here in this garden
　To drive away the heavy thought of care?
Lady
　Madam, we'll play at bowls.
Queen
　'Twill make me think the world is full of rubs
　And that my fortune runs against the bias.　　　　5
Lady
　Madam, we'll dance.
Queen
　My legs can keep no measure in delight,
　When my poor heart no measure keeps in grief;
　Therefore no dancing, girl; some other sport.
Lady
　Madam, we'll tell tales.　　　　　　　　　　　10
Queen
　Of sorrow or of joy?
Lady
　　　　　　　　Of either, madam.
Queen
　Of neither, girl;
　For if of joy, being altogether wanting,
　It doth remember me the more of sorrow;
　Or if of grief, being altogether had,　　　　　15
　It adds more sorrow to my want of joy;
　For what I have I need not to repeat,
　And what I want it boots not to complain.
Lady
　Madam, I'll sing.
Queen
　　　　　　　'Tis well that thou hast cause;

But thou shouldst please me better wouldst thou
20   weep.
  Lady
I could weep, madam, would it do you good.
  Queen
And I could sing, would weeping do me good,
And never borrow any tear of thee.

[Enter a Gardener and two Servants.]

But stay, here come the gardeners.
25   Let's step into the shadow of these trees.
My wretchedness unto a row of pins,
They will talk of state, for every one doth so
Against a change: woe is forerun with woe.

[QUEEN and Ladies retire.]

  Gardener
Go, bind thou up yon dangling apricocks,
30   Which, like unruly children, make their sire
Stoop with oppression of their prodigal weight;
Give some supportance to the bending twigs.
Go thou, and like an executioner
Cut off the heads of too fast growing sprays
35   That look too lofty in our commonwealth:
All must be even in our government.
You thus employ'd, I will go root away
The noisome weeds which without profit suck
The soil's fertility from wholesome flowers.
  Servant
40   Why should we, in the compass of a pale,
Keep law and form and due proportion,
Showing, as in a model, our firm estate,
When our sea-walled garden, the whole land,
Is full of weeds; her fairest flowers chok'd up,
45   Her fruit trees all unprun'd, her hedges ruin'd,
Her knots disordered, and her wholesome herbs
Swarming with caterpillars?

Gardener
                              Hold thy peace.
He that hath suffer'd this disorder'd spring
Hath now himself met with the fall of leaf;
The weeds which his broad-spreading leaves did
    shelter,   50
That seem'd in eating him to hold him up,
Are pluck'd up root and all by Boling-broke –
I mean the Earl of Wiltshire, Bushy, Green.

Servant
What, are they dead?

Gardener
                              They are; and Bolingbroke
Hath seiz'd the wasteful king. O, what pity is it   55
That he had not so trimm'd and dress'd his land
As we this garden! We at time of year
Do wound the bark, the skin of our fruit trees,
Lest, being over-proud in sap and blood,
With too much riches it confound itself;   60
Had he done so to great and growing men,
They might have liv'd to bear, and he to taste
Their fruits of duty. Superfluous branches
We lop away, that bearing boughs may live;
Had he done so, himself had borne the crown,   65
Which waste of idle hours hath quite thrown
    down.

Servant
What, think you the King shall be deposed?

Gardener
Depress'd he is already, and depos'd
'Tis doubt he will be. Letters came last night
To a dear friend of the good Duke of York's   70
That tell black tidings.

Queen
O, I am press'd to death through want of speaking!
    [Coming forward.]
Thou, old Adam's likeness, set to dress this garden,

How dares thy harsh rude tongue sound this
   unpleasing news?
75   What Eve, what serpent, hath suggested thee
To make a second fall of cursed man?
Why dost thou say King Richard is depos'd?
Dar'st thou, thou little better thing than earth,
Divine his downfall? Say, where, when, and how,
80   Cam'st thou by this ill tidings? Speak, thou wretch.
Gardener
Pardon me, madam; little joy have I
To breathe this news; yet what I say is true.
King Richard, he is in the mighty hold
Of Bolingbroke. Their fortunes both are weigh'd.
85   In your lord's scale is nothing but himself,
And some few vanities that make him light;
But in the balance of great Bolingbroke,
Besides himself, are all the English peers,
And with that odds he weighs King Richard down.
90   Post you to London, and you will find it so;
I speak no more than every one doth know.
Queen
Nimble mischance, that art so light of foot,
Doth not thy embassage belong to me,
And am I last that knows it? O, thou thinkest
95   To serve me last, that I may longest keep
Thy sorrow in my breast. Come, ladies, go
To meet at London London's king in woe.
What, was I born to this, that my sad look
Should grace the triumph of great Bolingbroke?
100   Gard'ner, for telling me these news of woe,
Pray God the plants thou graft'st may never grow!

[Exeunt QUEEN *and Ladies.]*

Gardener
Poor Queen, so that thy state might be no worse,
I would my skill were subject to thy curse.
Here did she fall a tear; here in this place

I'll set a bank of rue, sour herb of grace.   105
Rue, even for ruth, here shortly shall be seen,
In the remembrance of a weeping queen.

[Exeunt.]

ACT FOUR
Scene I

Westminster Hall.

[Enter, as to the Parliament, BOLINGBROKE, AUMERLE,
NORTHUMBERLAND, PERCY, FITZWATER, SURREY, *the*
BISHOP OF CARLISLE, *the* ABBOT OF WESTMINSTER,
and Others; Herald, Officers, and BAGOT.]

Bolingbroke
    Call forth Bagot.
    Now, Bagot, freely speak thy mind –
    What thou dost know of noble Gloucester's death;
    Who wrought it with the King, and who perform'd
5   The bloody office of his timeless end.
Bagot
    Then set before my face the Lord Aumerle.
Bolingbroke
    Cousin, stand forth, and look upon that man.
Bagot
    My Lord Aumerle, I know your daring tongue
    Scorns to unsay what once it hath deliver'd.
10   In that dead time when Gloucester's death was plotted
    I heard you say 'Is not my arm of length,
    That reacheth from the restful English Court
    As far as Calais, to mine uncle's head?'
    Amongst much other talk that very time
15   I heard you say that you had rather refuse
    The offer of an hundred thousand crowns
    Than Bolingbroke's return to England;
    Adding withal, how blest this land would be
    In this your cousin's death.
Aumerle
                   Princes, and noble lords,
20   What answer shall I make to this base man?

Shall I so much dishonour my fair stars
On equal terms to give him chastisement?
Either I must, or have mine honour soil'd
With the attainder of his slanderous lips.
There is my gage, the manual seal of death   25
That marks thee out for hell. I say thou liest,
And will maintain what thou hast said is false
In thy heart-blood, though being all too base
To stain the temper of my knightly sword.

Bolingbroke
Bagot, forbear; thou shalt not take it up.   30

Aumerle
Excepting one, I would he were the best
In all this presence that hath mov'd me so.

Fitzwater
If that thy valour stand on sympathy,
There is my gage, Aumerle, in gage to thine.
By that fair sun which shows me where thou
    stand'st,   35
I heard thee say, and vauntingly thou spak'st it,
That thou wert cause of noble Gloucester's death.
If thou deniest it twenty times, thou liest;
And I will turn thy falsehood to thy heart,
Where it was forged, with my rapier's point.   40

Aumerle
Thou dar'st not, coward, live to see that day.

Fitzwater
Now, by my soul, I would it were this hour.

Aumerle
Fitzwater, thou art damn'd to hell for this.

Percy
Aumerle, thou liest; his honour is as true
In this appeal as thou art all unjust;   45
And that thou art so, there I throw my gage,
To prove it on thee to the extremest point
Of mortal breathing. Seize it, if thou dar'st.

Aumerle
> An if I do not, may my hands rot off
50 > And never brandish more revengeful steel
> Over the glittering helmet of my foe!

Another lord
> I task the earth to the like, forsworn Aumerle;
> And spur thee on with full as many lies
> As may be holloa'd in thy treacherous ear
55 > From sun to sun. There is my honour's pawn;
> Engage it to the trial, if thou darest.

Aumerle
> Who sets me else? By heaven, I'll throw at all!
> I have a thousand spirits in one breast
> To answer twenty thousand such as you.

Surrey
60 > My Lord Fitzwater, I do remember well
> The very time Aumerle and you did talk.

Fitzwater
> 'Tis very true; you were in presence then,
> And you can witness with me this is true.

Surrey
> As false, by heaven, as heaven itself is true.

Fitzwater
> Surrey, thou liest.

Surrey
65 >   Dishonourable boy!
> That lie shall lie so heavy on my sword
> That it shall render vengeance and revenge
> Till thou the lie-giver and that lie do lie
> In earth as quiet as thy father's skull.
70 > In proof whereof, there is my honour's pawn;
> Engage it to the trial, if thou dar'st.

Fitzwater
> How fondly dost thou spur a forward horse!
> If I dare eat, or drink, or breathe, or live,
> I dare meet Surrey in a wilderness,
75 > And spit upon him whilst I say he lies,

And lies, and lies. There is my bond of faith,
To tie thee to my strong correction.
As I intend to thrive in this new world,
Aumerle is guilty of my true appeal.
Besides, I heard the banish'd Norfolk say   80
That thou, Aumerle, didst send two of thy men
To execute the noble Duke at Calais.

Aumerle

Some honest Christian trust me with a gage
That Norfolk lies. Here do I throw down this,
If he may be repeal'd to try his honour.   85

Bolingbroke

These differences shall all rest under gage
Till Norfolk be repeal'd – repeal'd shall be
And, though mine enemy, restor'd again
To all his lands and signories. When he is return'd,
Against Aumerle we will enforce his trial.   90

Carlisle

That honourable day shall never be seen.
Many a time hath banish'd Norfolk fought
For Jesu Christ in glorious Christian field,
Streaming the ensign of the Christian cross
Against black pagans, Turks, and Saracens;   95
And, toil'd with works of war, retir'd himself
To Italy; and there, at Venice, gave
His body to that pleasant country's earth,
And his pure soul unto his captain, Christ,
Under whose colours he had fought so long.   100

Bolingbroke

Why, Bishop, is Norfolk dead?

Carlisle

As surely as I live, my lord.

Bolingbroke

Sweet peace conduct his sweet soul to the bosom
Of good old Abraham! Lords appellants,
Your differences shall all rest under gage   105
Till we assign you to your days of trial.

[Enter YORK, attended.]

York

    Great Duke of Lancaster, I come to thee
    From plume-pluck'd Richard, who with willing soul
    Adopts thee heir, and his high sceptre yields
110   To the possession of thy royal hand.
    Ascend his throne, descending now from him –
    And long live Henry, fourth of that name!

Bolingbroke

    In God's name, I'll ascend the regal throne.

Carlisle

    Marry, God forbid!
115   Worst in this royal presence may I speak,
    Yet best beseeming me to speak the truth.
    Would God that any in this noble presence
    Were enough noble to be upright judge
    Of noble Richard! Then true noblesse would
120   Learn him forbearance from so foul a wrong.
    What subject can give sentence on his king?
    And who sits here that is not Richard's subject?
    Thieves are not judg'd but they are by to hear,
    Although apparent guilt be seen in them;
125   And shall the figure of God's majesty,
    His captain, steward, deputy elect,
    Anointed, crowned, planted many years,
    Be judg'd by subject and inferior breath,
    And he himself not present? O, forfend it, God,
130   That in a Christian climate souls refin'd
    Should show so heinous, black, obscene a deed!
    I speak to subjects, and a subject speaks,
    Stirr'd up by God, thus boldly for his king.
    My Lord of Hereford here, whom you call king,
135   Is a foul traitor to proud Hereford's king;
    And if you crown him, let me prophesy –
    The blood of English shall manure the ground,
    And future ages groan for this foul act;
    Peace shall go sleep with Turks and infidels,

And in this seat of peace tumultuous wars   140
Shall kin with kin and kind with kind confound;
Disorder, horror, fear, and mutiny,
Shall here inhabit, and this land be call'd
The field of Golgotha and dead men's skulls.
O, if you raise this house against this house,   145
It will the woefullest division prove
That ever fell upon this cursed earth.
Prevent it, resist it, let it not be so,
Lest child, child's children, cry against you woe.

Northumberland
Well have you argued, sir; and, for your pains,   150
Of capital treason we arrest you here.
My Lord of Westminster, be it your charge
To keep him safely till his day of trial.
May it please you, lords, to grant the commons'
    suit?

Bolingbroke
Fetch hither Richard, that in common view   155
He may surrender; so we shall proceed
Without suspicion.

York
              I will be his conduct. *[Exit.]*

Bolingbroke
Lords, you that here are under our arrest,
Procure your sureties for your days of answer.
Little are we beholding to your love,   160
And little look'd for at your helping hands.

    [Re-enter YORK, *with* KING RICHARD, *and Officers*
            bearing the regalia.]

King Richard
Alack, why am I sent for to a king,
Before I have shook off the regal thoughts
Wherewith I reign'd? I hardly yet have learn'd
To insinuate, flatter, bow, and bend my knee.   165
Give sorrow leave awhile to tutor me

To this submission. Yet I well remember
The favours of these men. Were they not mine?
Did they not sometime cry 'All hail!' to me?
170 So Judas did to Christ; but he, in twelve,
Found truth in all but one; I, in twelve thousand,
  none.
God save the King! Will no man say amen?
Am I both priest and clerk? Well then, amen.
God save the King! although I be not he;
175 And yet, amen, if heaven do think him me.
To do what service am I sent for hither?

York

To do that office of thine own good will
Which tired majesty did make thee offer –
The resignation of thy state and crown
180 To Henry Bolingbroke.

King Richard

Give me the crown. Here, cousin, seize the crown.
Here, cousin,
On this side my hand, and on that side thine.
Now is this golden crown like a deep well
185 That owes two buckets, filling one another;
The emptier ever dancing in the air,
The other down, unseen, and full of water.
That bucket down, and full of tears am I,
Drinking my griefs, whilst you mount up on high.

Bolingbroke

190 I thought you had been willing to resign.

King Richard

My crown I am; but still my griefs are mine.
You may my glories and my state depose,
But not my griefs; still am I king of those.

Bolingbroke

Part of your cares you give me with your crown.

King Richard

195 Your cares set up do not pluck my cares down.
My care is loss of care, by old care done;

Your care is gain of care, by new care won.
The cares I give I have, though given away;
They tend the crown, yet still with me they stay.

Bolingbroke

Are you contented to resign the crown?   200

King Richard

Ay, no; no, ay; for I must nothing be;
Therefore no no, for I resign to thee.
Now mark me how I will undo myself:
I give this heavy weight from off my head,
And this unwieldy sceptre from my hand,   205
The pride of kingly sway from out my heart;
With mine own tears I wash away my balm,
With mine own hands I give away my crown,
With mine own tongue deny my sacred state,
With mine own breath release all duteous oaths;   210
All pomp and majesty I do forswear;
My manors, rents, revenues, I forgo;
My acts, decrees, and statutes, I deny.
God pardon all oaths that are broke to me!
God keep all vows unbroke are made to thee!   215
Make me, that nothing have, with nothing griev'd,
And thou with all pleas'd, that hast all achiev'd.
Long mayst thou live in Richard's seat to sit,
And soon lie Richard in an earthy pit.
God save King Henry, unking'd Richard says,   220
And send him many years of sunshine days!
What more remains?

Northumberland

                              No more; but that you read
These accusations, and these grievous crimes
Committed by your person and your followers
Against the state and profit of this land;   225
That, by confessing them, the souls of men
May deem that you are worthily depos'd.

King Richard

Must I do so? And must I ravel out

85

My weav'd-up follies? Gentle Northumberland,
230 If thy offences were upon record,
Would it not shame thee in so fair a troop
To read a lecture of them? If thou wouldst,
There shouldst thou find one heinous article,
Containing the deposing of a king
235 And cracking the strong warrant of an oath,
Mark'd with a blot, damn'd in the book of heaven.
Nay, all of you that stand and look upon me
Whilst that my wretchedness doth bait myself,
Though some of you, with Pilate, wash your hands,
240 Showing an outward pity – yet you Pilates
Have here deliver'd me to my sour cross,
And water cannot wash away your sin.

Northumberland
My lord, dispatch; read o'er these articles.

King Richard
Mine eyes are full of tears; I cannot see.
245 And yet salt water blinds them not so much
But they can see a sort of traitors here.
Nay, if I turn mine eyes upon myself,
I find myself a traitor with the rest;
For I have given here my soul's consent
250 T' undeck the pompous body of a king;
Made glory base, and sovereignty a slave,
Proud majesty a subject, state a peasant.

Northumberland
My lord –

King Richard
No lord of thine, thou haught insulting man,
255 Nor no man's lord; I have no name, no title –
No, not that name was given me at the font –
But 'tis usurp'd. Alack the heavy day,
That I have worn so many winters out,
And know not now what name to call myself!
260 O that I were a mockery king of snow,
Standing before the sun of Bolingbroke

To melt myself away in water drops!
Good king, great king, and yet not greatly good,
An if my word be sterling yet in England,
Let it command a mirror hither straight,   265
That it may show me what a face I have
Since it is bankrupt of his majesty.

Bolingbroke
Go some of you and fetch a looking-glass.
    [Exit an Attendant.]

Northumberland
Read o'er this paper while the glass doth come.

King Richard
Fiend, thou torments me ere I come to hell.   270

Bolingbroke
Urge it no more, my Lord Northumberland.

Northumberland
The commons will not, then, be satisfied.

King Richard
They shall be satisfied. I'll read enough,
When I do see the very book indeed
Where all my sins are writ, and that's myself.   275

    [Re-enter Attendant with a glass.]

Give me that glass, and therein will I read.
No deeper wrinkles yet? Hath sorrow struck
So many blows upon this face of mine
And made no deeper wounds? O flatt'ring glass,
Like to my followers in prosperity,   280
Thou dost beguile me! Was this face the face
That every day under his household roof
Did keep ten thousand men? Was this the face
That like the sun did make beholders wink?
Is this the face which fac'd so many follies   285
That was at last out-fac'd by Bolingbroke?
A brittle glory shineth in this face;
As brittle as the glory is the face;

    [Dashes the glass against the ground.]

For there it is, crack'd in a hundred shivers.
290   Mark, silent king, the moral of this sport –
How soon my sorrow hath destroy'd my face.
Bolingbroke
The shadow of your sorrow hath destroy'd
The shadow of your face.
King Richard
                              Say that again.
The shadow of my sorrow? Ha! let's see.
295   'Tis very true: my grief lies all within;
And these external manner of laments
Are merely shadows to the unseen grief
That swells with silence in the tortur'd soul.
There lies the substance; and I thank thee, king,
300   For thy great bounty, that not only giv'st
Me cause to wail, but teachest me the way
How to lament the cause. I'll beg one boon,
And then be gone and trouble you no more.
Shall I obtain it?
Bolingbroke
                    Name it, fair cousin.
King Richard
305   Fair cousin! I am greater than a king;
For when I was a king, my flatterers
Were then but subjects; being now a subject,
I have a king here to my flatterer.
Being so great, I have no need to beg.
Bolingbroke
310   Yet ask.
King Richard
And shall I have?
Bolingbroke
You shall.
King Richard
Then give me leave to go.
Bolingbroke
Whither?

King Richard
> Whither you will, so I were from your sights. 315
Bolingbroke
> Go, some of you convey him to the Tower.
King Richard
> O, good! Convey! Conveyers are you all,
> That rise thus nimbly by a true king's fall.

> *[Exeunt KING RICHARD, some Lords, and a Guard.]*

Bolingbroke
> On Wednesday next we solemnly set down
> Our coronation. Lords, prepare yourselves. 320

> *[Exeunt all but the ABBOT OF WESTMINSTER, the*
> *BISHOP OF CARLISLE, and AUMERLE.]*

Abbot
> A woeful pageant have we here beheld.
Carlisle
> The woe's to come; the children yet unborn
> Shall feel this day as sharp to them as thorn.
Aumerle
> You holy clergymen, is there no plot
> To rid the realm of this pernicious blot? 325
Abbot
> My lord,
> Before I freely speak my mind herein,
> You shall not only take the sacrament
> To bury mine intents, but also to effect
> Whatever I shall happen to devise. 330
> I see your brows are full of discontent,
> Your hearts of sorrow, and your eyes of tears.
> Come home with me to supper; I will lay
> A plot shall show us all a merry day. *[Exeunt.]*

ACT FIVE
Scene I

London. A street leading to the Tower.

[Enter the QUEEN, with her Attendants.]

Queen

This way the King will come; this is the way
To Julius Caesar's ill-erected tower,
To whose flint bosom my condemned lord
Is doom'd a prisoner by proud Bolingbroke.
5   Here let us rest, if this rebellious earth
Have any resting for her true king's queen.

[Enter KING RICHARD and Guard.]

But soft, but see, or rather do not see,
My fair rose wither. Yet look up, behold,
That you in pity may dissolve to dew,
10   And wash him fresh again with true-love tears.
Ah, thou, the model where old Troy did stand;
Thou map of honour, thou King Richard's tomb,
And not King Richard; thou most beauteous inn,
Why should hard-favour'd grief be lodg'd in thee,
15   When triumph is become an alehouse guest?

King Richard

Join not with grief, fair woman, do not so,
To make my end too sudden. Learn, good soul,
To think our former state a happy dream;
From which awak'd, the truth of what we are
20   Shows us but this: I am sworn brother, sweet,
To grim Necessity; and he and I
Will keep a league till death. Hie thee to France,
And cloister thee in some religious house.

Our holy lives must win a new world's crown,
Which our profane hours here have thrown down.   25

Queen

What, is my Richard both in shape and mind
Transform'd and weak'ned? Hath Bolingbroke depos'd
Thine intellect? Hath he been in thy heart?
The lion dying thrusteth forth his paw
And wounds the earth, if nothing else, with rage   30
To be o'erpow'r'd; and wilt thou, pupil-like,
Take the correction mildly, kiss the rod,
And fawn on rage with base humility,
Which art a lion and the king of beasts?

King Richard

A king of beasts, indeed! If aught but beasts,   35
I had been still a happy king of men.
Good sometimes queen, prepare thee hence for
    France.
Think I am dead, and that even here thou takest,
As from my death-bed, thy last living leave.
In winter's tedious nights sit by the fire   40
With good old folks, and let them tell thee tales
Of woeful ages long ago betid;
And ere thou bid good night, to quit their griefs
Tell thou the lamentable tale of me,
And send the hearers weeping to their beds;   45
For why the senseless brands will sympathize
The heavy accent of thy moving tongue,
And in compassion weep the fire out;
And some will mourn in ashes, some coal-black,
For the deposing of a rightful king.   50

[Enter NORTHUMBERLAND attended.]

Northumberland

My lord, the mind of Bolingbroke is chang'd;
You must to Pomfret, not unto the Tower.
And, madam, there is order ta'en for you:
With all swift speed you must away to France.

King Richard

55   Northumberland, thou ladder wherewithal
    The mounting Bolingbroke ascends my throne,
    The time shall not be many hours of age
    More than it is, ere foul sin gathering head
    Shall break into corruption. Thou shalt think
60   Though he divide the realm and give thee half
    It is too little, helping him to all;
    And he shall think that thou, which knowest the
        way
    To plant unrightful kings, wilt know again,
    Being ne'er so little urg'd, another way
65   To pluck him headlong from the usurped throne.
    The love of wicked men converts to fear;
    That fear to hate; and hate turns one or both
    To worthy danger and deserved death.

Northumberland

    My guilt be on my head, and there an end.
70   Take leave, and part; for you must part forthwith.

King Richard

    Doubly divorc'd! Bad men, you violate
    A twofold marriage – 'twixt my crown and me,
    And then betwixt me and my married wife.
    Let me unkiss the oath 'twixt thee and me;
75   And yet not so, for with a kiss 'twas made.
    Part us, Northumberland; I towards the north,
    Where shivering cold and sickness pines the clime;
    My wife to France, from whence set forth in pomp,
    She came adorned hither like sweet May,
80   Sent back like Hallowmas or short'st of day.

Queen

    And must we be divided? Must we part?

King Richard

    Ay, hand from hand, my love, and heart from heart.

Queen

    Banish us both, and send the King with me.

Northumberland
    That were some love, but little policy.
Queen
    Then whither he goes thither let me go.   85
King Richard
    So two, together weeping, make one woe.
    Weep thou for me in France, I for thee here;
    Better far off than near, be ne'er the near.
    Go, count thy way with sighs; I mine with groans.
Queen
    So longest way shall have the longest moans.   90
King Richard
    Twice for one step I'll groan, the way being short,
    And piece the way out with a heavy heart.
    Come, come, in wooing sorrow let's be brief,
    Since, wedding it, there is such length in grief.
    One kiss shall stop our mouths, and dumbly part;   95
    Thus give I mine, and thus take I thy heart.
Queen
    Give me mine own again; 'twere no good part
    To take on me to keep and kill thy heart.
    So, now I have mine own again, be gone,
    That I may strive to kill it with a groan.   100
King Richard
    We make woe wanton with this fond delay.
    Once more, adieu; the rest let sorrow say.

                        [Exeunt.]

Scene II

The Duke of York's palace.

[*Enter the* DUKE OF YORK *and the* DUCHESS.]

Duchess
My lord, you told me you would tell the rest,
When weeping made you break the story off,
Of our two cousins' coming into London.

York
Where did I leave?

Duchess
            At that sad stop, my lord,
5   Where rude misgoverned hands from windows' tops
Threw dust and rubbish on King Richard's head.

York
Then, as I said, the Duke, great Bolingbroke,
Mounted upon a hot and fiery steed
Which his aspiring rider seem'd to know,
10 With slow but stately pace kept on his course,
Whilst all tongues cried 'God save thee, Bolingbroke!'
You would have thought the very windows spake,
So many greedy looks of young and old
Through casements darted their desiring eyes
15 Upon his visage; and that all the walls
With painted imagery had said at once
'Jesu preserve thee! Welcome, Bolingbroke!'
Whilst he, from the one side to the other turning,
Bareheaded, lower than his proud steed's neck,
20 Bespake them thus, 'I thank you, countrymen'.
And thus still doing, thus he pass'd along.

Duchess
Alack, poor Richard! where rode he the whilst?

York
As in a theatre the eyes of men
After a well-grac'd actor leaves the stage
25 Are idly bent on him that enters next,

Thinking his prattle to be tedious;
Even so, or with much more contempt, men's eyes
Did scowl on gentle Richard; no man cried 'God
    save him!'
No joyful tongue gave him his welcome home;
But dust was thrown upon his sacred head;   30
Which with such gentle sorrow he shook off,
His face still combating with tears and smiles,
The badges of his grief and patience,
That had not God, for some strong purpose, steel'd
The hearts of men, they must perforce have melted,   35
And barbarism itself have pitied him.
But heaven hath a hand in these events,
To whose high will we bound our calm contents.
To Bolingbroke are we sworn subjects now,
Whose state and honour I for aye allow.   40
Duchess
Here comes my son Aumerle.
York
                      Aumerle that was;
But that is lost for being Richard's friend,
And, madam, you must call him Rutland now.
I am in Parliament pledge for his truth
And lasting fealty to the new-made king.   45

[Enter AUMERLE.]

Duchess
Welcome, my son. Who are the violets now
That strew the green lap of the new come spring?
Aumerle
Madam, I know not, nor I greatly care not.
God knows I had as lief be none as one.
York
Well, bear you well in this new spring of time,   50
Lest you be cropp'd before you come to prime.
What news from Oxford? Do these justs and
    triumphs hold?

Aumerle
> For aught I know, my lord, they do.

York
> You will be there, I know.

Aumerle
55   If God prevent not, I purpose so.

York
> What seal is that that hangs without thy bosom?
> Yea, look'st thou pale? Let me see the writing.

Aumerle
> My lord, 'tis nothing.

York
>   No matter, then, who see it.
> I will be satisfied; let me see the writing.

Aumerle
60   I do beseech your Grace to pardon me;
> It is a matter of small consequence
> Which for some reasons I would not have seen.

York
> Which for some reasons, sir, I mean to see.
> I fear, I fear –

Duchess
>   What should you fear?
65   'Tis nothing but some bond that he is ent'red into
> For gay apparel 'gainst the triumph-day.

York
> Bound to himself! What doth he with a bond
> That he is bound to? Wife, thou art a fool.
> Boy, let me see the writing.

Aumerle
70   I do beseech you, pardon me; I may not show it.

York
> I will be satisfied; let me see it, I say.

[He plucks it out of his bosom, and reads it.]

Treason, foul treason! Villain! traitor! slave!

Duchess
    What is the matter, my lord?
York
    Ho! who is within there?

            [Enter a Servant.]

                Saddle my horse.
    God for his mercy, what treachery is here!   75
Duchess
    Why, what is it, my lord?
York
      Give me my boots, I say; saddle my horse.

            [Exit Servant.]

    Now, by mine honour, by my life, my troth,
    I will appeach the villain.
Duchess
                  What is the matter?
York
    Peace, foolish woman.   80
Duchess
    I will not peace. What is the matter, Aumerle?
Aumerle
    Good mother, be content; it is no more
    Than my poor life must answer.
Duchess
                Thy life answer!
York
    Bring me my boots. I will unto the King.

        [His Man enters with his boots.]

Duchess
    Strike him, Aumerle. Poor boy, thou art amaz'd.   85
    Hence, villain! never more come in my sight.
York
    Give me my boots, I say.

Duchess
Why, York, what wilt thou do?
Wilt thou not hide the trespass of thine own?
90   Have we more sons? or are we like to have?
Is not my teeming date drunk up with time?
And wilt thou pluck my fair son from mine age
And rob me of a happy mother's name?
Is he not like thee? Is he not thine own?

York
95   Thou fond mad woman,
Wilt thou conceal this dark conspiracy?
A dozen of them here have ta'en the sacrament,
And interchangeably set down their hands
To kill the King at Oxford.

Duchess
                      He shall be none;
100   We'll keep him here. Then what is that to him?

York
Away fond woman! were he twenty times my son
I would appeach him.

Duchess
               Hadst thou groan'd for him
As I have done, thou wouldst be more pitiful.
But now I know thy mind: thou dost suspect
105   That I have been disloyal to thy bed
And that he is a bastard, not thy son.
Sweet York, sweet husband, be not of that mind.
He is as like thee as a man may be,
Not like to me, or any of my kin,
And yet I love him.

York
110   Make way, unruly woman!

[Exit.]

Duchess
After, Aumerle! Mount thee upon his horse;
Spur post, and get before him to the King,

And beg thy pardon ere he do accuse thee.
I'll not be long behind; though I be old,
I doubt not but to ride as fast as York;   115
And never will I rise up from the ground
Till Bolingbroke have pardon'd thee. Away, be gone.

[Exeunt.]

Scene III

Windsor Castle.

[Enter BOLINGBROKE as King, PERCY, and other Lords.]

Bolingbroke

    Can no man tell me of my unthrifty son?
    'Tis full three months since I did see him last.
    If any plague hang over us, 'tis he.
    I would to God, my lords, he might be found.
5   Inquire at London, 'mongst the taverns there,
    For there, they say, he daily doth frequent
    With unrestrained loose companions,
    Even such, they say, as stand in narrow lanes
    And beat our watch and rob our passengers,
10   Which he, young wanton and effeminate boy,
    Takes on the point of honour to support
    So dissolute a crew.

Percy

    My lord, some two days since I saw the Prince,
    And told him of those triumphs held at Oxford.

Bolingbroke

15   And what said the gallant?

Percy

    His answer was, he would unto the stews,
    And from the common'st creature pluck a glove
    And wear it as a favour; and with that
    He would unhorse the lustiest challenger.

Bolingbroke

20   As dissolute as desperate; yet through both
    I see some sparks of better hope, which elder years
    May happily bring forth. But who comes here?

[Enter AUMERLE amazed.]

Aumerle

    Where is the King?

Bolingbroke
What means our cousin that he stares and looks
So wildly?   25
Aumerle
God save your Grace! I do beseech your Majesty,
To have some conference with your Grace alone.
Bolingbroke
Withdraw yourselves, and leave us here alone.

[Exeunt PERCY *and Lords.]*

What is the matter with our cousin now?

Aumerle
For ever may my knees grow to the earth,   30
    [Kneels.]
My tongue cleave to my roof within my mouth,
Unless a pardon ere I rise or speak.
Bolingbroke
Intended or committed was this fault?
If on the first, how heinous e'er it be,
To win thy after-love I pardon thee.   35
Aumerle
Then give me leave that I may turn the key,
That no man enter till my tale be done.
Bolingbroke
Have thy desire.

[The DUKE OF YORK *knocks at the door and crieth.]*

York
[Within] My liege, beware; look to thyself;
Thou hast a traitor in thy presence there.   40
Bolingbroke
[Drawing] Villain, I'll make thee safe.
Aumerle
Stay thy revengeful hand; thou hast no cause to fear.
York
[Within] Open the door, secure, foolhardy King.

Shall I, for love, speak treason to thy face?
45 Open the door, or I will break it open.

[Enter YORK.]

Bolingbroke
What is the matter, uncle? Speak;
Recover breath; tell us how near is danger,
That we may arm us to encounter it.
York
Peruse this writing here, and thou shalt know
50 The treason that my haste forbids me show.
Aumerle
Remember, as thou read'st, thy promise pass'd.
I do repent me; read not my name there;
My heart is not confederate with my hand.
York
It was, villain, ere thy hand did set it down.
55 I tore it from the traitor's bosom, King;
Fear, and not love, begets his penitence.
Forget to pity him, lest thy pity prove
A serpent that will sting thee to the heart.
Bolingbroke
O heinous, strong, and bold conspiracy!
60 O loyal father of a treacherous son!
Thou sheer, immaculate, and silver fountain,
From whence this stream through muddy passages
Hath held his current and defil'd himself!
Thy overflow of good converts to bad;
65 And thy abundant goodness shall excuse
This deadly blot in thy digressing son.
York
So shall my virtue be his vice's bawd;
And he shall spend mine honour with his shame,
As thriftless sons their scraping fathers' gold.
70 Mine honour lives when his dishonour dies,
Or my sham'd life in his dishonour lies.
Thou kill'st me in his life; giving him breath,

The traitor lives, the true man's put to death.

Duchess

[Within] What ho, my liege, for God's sake, let me in.

Bolingbroke

What shrill-voic'd suppliant makes this eager cry?   75

Duchess

[Within] A woman, and thin aunt, great King; 'tis I.
Speak with me, pity me, open the door.
A beggar begs that never begg'd before.

Bolingbroke

Our scene is alt'red from a serious thing,
And now chang'd to 'The Beggar and the King'.   80
My dangerous cousin, let your mother in.
I know she is come to pray for your foul sin.

York

If thou do pardon whosoever pray,
More sins for this forgiveness prosper may.
This fest'red joint cut off, the rest rest sound;   85
This let alone will all the rest confound.

[Enter DUCHESS.]

Duchess

O King, believe not this hard-hearted man!
Love loving not itself, none other can.

York

Thou frantic woman, what dost thou make here?
Shall thy old dugs once more a traitor rear?   90

Duchess

Sweet York, be patient. Hear me, gentle liege.
    [Kneels.]

Bolingbroke

Rise up, good aunt.

Duchess

                    Not yet, I thee beseech.
For ever will I walk upon my knees,
And never see day that the happy sees
Till thou give joy; until thou bid me joy   95

By pardoning Rutland, my transgressing boy.

Aumerle

Unto my mother's prayers I bend my knee.
   [Kneels.]

York

Against them both, my true joints bended be.
   [Kneels.]

Ill mayst thou thrive, if thou grant any grace!

Duchess

100 Pleads he in earnest? Look upon his face;
His eyes do drop no tears, his prayers are in jest;
His words come from his mouth, ours from our
   breast.
He prays but faintly and would be denied;
We pray with heart and soul, and all beside.

105 His weary joints would gladly rise, I know;
Our knees still kneel till to the ground they grow.
His prayers are full of false hypocrisy;
Ours of true zeal and deep integrity.
Our prayers do out-pray his; then let them have

110 That mercy which true prayer ought to have.

Bolingbroke

Good aunt, stand up.

Duchess

                Nay, do not say 'stand up';
Say 'pardon' first, and afterwards 'stand up'.
An if I were thy nurse, thy tongue to teach,
'Pardon' should be the first word of thy speech.

115 I never long'd to hear a word till now;
Say 'pardon' King; let pity teach thee how.
The word is short, but not so short as sweet;
No word like 'pardon' for kings' mouths so meet.

York

Speak it in French, King, say 'pardonne moy'.

Duchess

120 Dost thou teach pardon pardon to destroy?
Ah, my sour husband, my hard-hearted lord,

That sets the word itself against the word!
Speak 'pardon' as 'tis current in our land;
The chopping French we do not understand.
Thine eye begins to speak, set thy tongue there;   125
Or in thy piteous heart plant thou thine ear,
That hearing how our plaints and prayers do pierce,
Pity may move thee 'pardon' to rehearse.

Bolingbroke

Good aunt, stand up.

Duchess

              I do not sue to stand;
Pardon is all the suit I have in hand.   130

Bolingbroke

I pardon him, as God shall pardon me.

Duchess

O happy vantage of a kneeling knee!
Yet am I sick for fear. Speak it again.
Twice saying 'pardon' doth not pardon twain,
But makes one pardon strong.

Bolingbroke

                With all my heart   135
I pardon him.

Duchess

           A god on earth thou art.

Bolingbroke

But for our trusty brother-in-law and the Abbot,
With all the rest of that consorted crew,
Destruction straight shall dog them at the heels.
Good uncle, help to order several powers   140
To Oxford, or where'er these traitors are.
They shall not live within this world, I swear,
But I will have them, if I once know where.
Uncle, farewell; and, cousin, adieu;
Your mother well hath pray'd, and prove you true.   145

Duchess

Come, my old son; I pray God make thee new.

[Exeunt.]

Scene IV

Windsor Castle.

[Enter SIR PIERCE OF EXTON *and a Servant.]*

Exton
  Didst thou not mark the King, what words he spake?
  'Have I no friend will rid me of this living fear?'
  Was it not so?

Servant
                    These were his very words.

Exton
  'Have I no friend?' quoth he. He spake it twice,
5 And urg'd it twice together, did he not?

Servant
  He did.

Exton
  And, speaking it, he wishtly look'd on me,
  As who should say 'I would thou wert the man
  That would divorce this terror from my heart';
10 Meaning the king at Pomfret. Come, let's go.
  I am the King's friend, and will rid his foe.

[Exeunt.]

Scene V

Pomfret Castle. The dungeon of the Castle.

[Enter KING RICHARD.]

King Richard
    I have been studying how I may compare
    This prison where I live unto the world;
    And, for because the world is populous
    And here is not a creature but myself,
    I cannot do it. Yet I'll hammer it out.   5
    My brain I'll prove the female to my soul,
    My soul the father; and these two beget
    A generation of still-breeding thoughts,
    And these same thoughts people this little world,
    In humours like the people of this world,   10
    For no thought is contented. The better sort,
    As thoughts of things divine, are inter-mix'd
    With scruples, and do set the word itself
    Against the word,
    As thus: 'Come, little ones'; and then again,   15
    'It is as hard to come as for a camel
    To thread the postern of a small needle's eye'.
    Thoughts tending to ambition, they do plot
    Unlikely wonders: how these vain weak nails
    May tear a passage through the flinty ribs   20
    Of this hard world, my ragged prison walls;
    And, for they cannot, die in their own pride.
    Thoughts tending to content flatter themselves
    That they are not the first of fortune's slaves,
    Nor shall not be the last; like silly beggars   25
    Who, sitting in the stocks, refuge their shame,
    That many have and others must sit there;
    And in this thought they find a kind of ease,
    Bearing their own misfortunes on the back
    Of such as have before endur'd the like.   30
    Thus play I in one person many people,

And none contented. Sometimes am I king;
Then treasons make me wish myself a beggar,
And so I am. Then crushing penury
35   Persuades me I was better when a king;
Then am I king'd again; and by and by
Think that I am unking'd by Bolingbroke,
And straight am nothing. But whate'er I be,
Nor I, nor any man that but man is,
40   With nothing shall be pleas'd till he be eas'd
With being nothing.

[The music plays.]

Music do I hear?
Ha, ha! keep time. How sour sweet music is
When time is broke and no proportion kept!
So is it in the music of men's lives.
45   And here have I the daintiness of ear
To check time broke in a disorder'd string;
But, for the concord of my state and time,
Had not an ear to hear my true time broke.
I wasted time, and now doth time waste me;
50   For now hath time made me his numb'ring clock:
My thoughts are minutes; and with sighs they jar
Their watches on unto mine eyes, the outward
    watch.
Whereto my finger, like a dial's point,
Is pointing still, in cleansing them from tears.
55   Now, sir, the sound that tells what hour it is
Are clamorous groans which strike upon my heart,
Which is the bell. So sighs, and tears, and groans,
Show minutes, times, and hours; but my time
Runs posting on in Bolingbroke's proud joy,
60   While I stand fooling here, his Jack of the clock.
This music mads me. Let it sound no more;
For though it have holp madmen to their wits,
In me it seems it will make wise men mad.
Yet blessing on his heart that gives it me!

For 'tis a sign of love; and love to Richard   65
Is a strange brooch in this all-hating world.

[Enter a Groom of the stable.]

Groom

Hail, royal Prince!

King Richard

                Thanks, noble peer!
The cheapest of us is ten groats too dear.
What art thou? and how comest thou hither,
Where no man never comes but that sad dog   70
That brings me food to make misfortune live?

Groom

I was a poor groom of thy stable, King,
When thou wert king; who, travelling towards York,
With much ado at length have gotten leave
To look upon my sometimes royal master's face.   75
O, how it ern'd my heart, when I beheld,
In London streets, that coronation-day,
When Bolingbroke rode on roan Barbary –
That horse that thou so often hast bestrid,
That horse that I so carefully have dress'd!   80

King Richard

Rode he on Barbary? Tell me, gentle friend,
How went he under him?

Groom

So proudly as if he disdain'd the ground.

King Richard

So proud that Bolingbroke was on his back!
That jade hath eat bread from my royal hand;   85
This hand hath made him proud with clapping him.
Would he not stumble? would he not fall down,
Since pride must have a fall, and break the neck
Of that proud man that did usurp his back?
Forgiveness, horse! Why do I rail on thee,   90
Since thou, created to be aw'd by man,
Wast born to bear? I was not made a horse;

And yet I bear a burden like an ass,
Spurr'd, gall'd, and tir'd, by jauncing Bolingbroke.

[Enter Keeper with meat.]

Keeper
95   Fellow, give place; here is no longer stay.
King Richard
If thou love me, 'tis time thou wert away.
Groom
What my tongue dares not, that my heart shall say.
    [Exit.]
Keeper
My lord, will't please you to fall to?
King Richard
Taste of it first as thou art wont to do.
Keeper
100   My lord, I dare not. Sir Pierce of Exton,
Who lately came from the King, commands the
    contrary.
King Richard
The devil take Henry of Lancaster and thee!
Patience is stale, and I am weary of it.

[Beats the Keeper.]

Keeper
Help, help, help!

[The murderers, EXTON and Servants, rush in, armed.]

King Richard
105   How now! What means death in this rude assault?
Villain, thy own hand yields thy death's instrument.

[Snatching a weapon and killing one.]

Go thou and fill another room in hell.

[He kills another, then EXTON strikes him down.]

That hand shall burn in never-quenching fire

That staggers thus my person. Exton, thy fierce hand
Hath with the King's blood stain'd the King's own
   land.   110
Mount, mount, my soul! thy seat is up on high;
Whilst my gross flesh sinks downward, here to die.
   [Dies.]

Exton

As full of valour as of royal blood.
Both have I spill'd. O, would the deed were good!
For now the devil, that told me I did well,   115
Says that this deed is chronicled in hell.
This dead king to the living king I'll bear.
Take hence the rest, and give them burial here.

                [Exeunt.]

Scene VI

Windsor Castle.

[Flourish. Enter BOLINGBROKE, *the* DUKE OF YORK, *with
other Lords and Attendants.]*

Bolingbroke
>Kind uncle York, the latest news we hear
>Is that the rebels have consum'd with fire
>Our town of Ciceter in Gloucestershire;
>But whether they be ta'en or slain we hear not.

[Enter NORTHUMBERLAND.*]*

5 Welcome, my lord. What is the news?
Northumberland
>First, to thy sacred state wish I all happiness.
>The next news is, I have to London sent
>The heads of Salisbury, Spencer, Blunt, and Kent.
>The manner of their taking may appear
>10 At large discoursed in this paper here.
Bolingbroke
>We thank thee, gentle Percy, for thy pains;
>And to thy worth will add right worthy gains.

[Enter FITZWATER.*]*

Fitzwater
>My lord, I have from Oxford sent to London
>The heads of Brocas and Sir Bennet Seely;
>15 Two of the dangerous consorted traitors
>That sought at Oxford thy dire overthrow.
Bolingbroke
>Thy pains, Fitzwater, shall not be forgot;
>Right noble is thy merit, well I wot.

[Enter PERCY, *with the* BISHOP OF CARLISLE.*]*

Percy
>The grand conspirator, Abbot of Westminster,

With clog of conscience and sour melancholy,   20
Hath yielded up his body to the grave;
But here is Carlisle living, to abide
Thy kingly doom, and sentence of his pride.

Bolingbroke

Carlisle, this is your doom:
Choose out some secret place, some reverend room,   25
More than thou hast, and with it joy thy life;
So as thou liv'st in peace, die free from strife;
For though mine enemy thou hast ever been,
High sparks of honour in thee have I seen.

[Enter EXTON, with Attendants, bearing a coffin.]

Exton

Great King, within this coffin I present   30
Thy buried fear. Herein all breathless lies
The mightiest of thy greatest enemies,
Richard of Bordeaux, by me hither brought.

Bolingbroke

Exton, I thank thee not; for thou hast wrought
A deed of slander with thy fatal hand   35
Upon my head and all this famous land.

Exton

From your own mouth, my lord, did I this deed.

Bolingbroke

They love not poison that do poison need,
Nor do I thee. Though I did wish him dead,
I hate the murderer, love him murdered.   40
The guilt of conscience take thou for thy labour,
But neither my good word nor princely favour;
With Cain go wander thorough shades of night,
And never show thy head by day nor light.
Lords, I protest my soul is full of woe   45
That blood should sprinkle me to make me grow.
Come, mourn with me for what I do lament,
And put on sullen black incontinent.
I'll make a voyage to the Holy Land,

50   To wash this blood off from my guilty hand.
      March sadly after; grace my mournings here
      In weeping after this untimely bier.

[Exeunt.]

Shakespeare: Words and Phrases

adapted from the Collins English Dictionary

abate 1 VERB to abate here means to lessen or diminish ❏ *There lives within the very flame of love/A kind of wick or snuff that will abate it* (*Hamlet 4.7*) 2 VERB to abate here means to shorten ❏ *Abate thy hours* (*A Midsummer Night's Dream 3.2*) 3 VERB to abate here means to deprive ❏ *She hath abated me of half my train* (*King Lear 2.4*)

abjure VERB to abjure means to renounce or give up ❏ *this rough magic I here abjure* (*Tempest 5.1*)

abroad ADV abroad means elsewhere or everywhere ❏ *You have heard of the news abroad* (*King Lear 2.1*)

abrogate VERB to abrogate means to put an end to ❏ *so it shall praise you to abrogate scurrility* (*Love's Labours Lost 4.2*)

abuse 1 NOUN abuse in this context means deception or fraud ❏ *What should this mean? Are all the rest come back?/Or is it some abuse, and no such thing?* (*Hamlet 4.7*) 2 NOUN an abuse in this context means insult or offence ❏ *I will be deaf to pleading and excuses/Nor tears nor prayers shall purchase our abuses* (*Romeo and Juliet 3.1*) 3 NOUN an abuse in this context means using something improperly ❏ *we'll digest/Th'abuse*

of distance (*Henry II Chorus*) 4 NOUN an abuse in this context means doing something which is corrupt or dishonest ❏ *Come, bring them away: if these be good people in a commonweal that do nothing but their abuses in common houses, I know no law: bring them away.* (*Measure for Measure 2.1*)

abuser NOUN the abuser here is someone who betrays, a betrayer ❏ *I ... do attach thee/For an abuser of the world* (*Othello 1.2*)

accent NOUN accent here means language ❏ *In states unborn, and accents yet unknown* (*Julius Caesar 3.1*)

accident NOUN an accident in this context is an event or something that happened ❏ *think no more of this night's accidents* (*A Midsummer Night's Dream 4.1*)

accommodate VERB to accommodate in this context means to equip or to give someone the equipment to do something ❏ *The safer sense will ne'er accommodate/His master thus.* (*King Lear 4.6*)

according ADJ according means sympathetic or ready to agree ❏ *within the scope of choice/Lies*

my consent and fair according voice
(*Romeo and Juliet 1.2*)

account NOUN account often means
judgement (by God) or reckoning
❏ *No reckoning made, but sent to my
account/ With all my imperfections on
my head* (*Hamlet 1.5*)

accountant ADJ accountant here
means answerable or accountable
❏ *his offence is… /Accountant to the
law* (*Measure for Measure 2.4*)

ace NOUN ace here means one or first
referring to the lowest score on a dice
❏ *No die, but an ace, for him; for he is
but one./Less than an ace, man; for he
is dead; he is nothing.* (*A Midsummer
Night's Dream 5.1*)

acquit VERB here acquit means to be
rid of or free of. It is related to the
verb quit ❏ *I am glad I am so acquit
of this tinderbox* (*The Merry Wives of
Windsor 1.3*)

afeard ADJ afeard means afraid or
frightened ❏ *Nothing afeard of what
thyself didst make* (*Macbeth 1.3*)

affiance NOUN affiance means
confidence or trust ❏ *O how hast
thou with jealousy infected/ The
sweetness of affiance* (*Henry V 2.2*)

affinity NOUN in this context, affinity
means important connections, or
relationships with important people
❏ *The Moor replies/ That he you hurt
is of great fame in Cyprus,/ And great
affinity* (*Othello 3.1*)

agnize VERB to agnize is an old
word that means that you recognize
or acknowledge something ❏ *I do
agnize/ A natural and prompt alacrity
I find in hardness* (*Othello 1.3*)

ague NOUN an ague is a fever in
which the patient has hot and cold

shivers one after the other ❏ *This
is some monster of the isle with four
legs, who hath got … an ague* (*The
Tempest 2.2*)

alarm, alarum NOUN an alarm or
alarum is a call to arms or a signal for
soldiers to prepare to fight ❏ *Whence
cometh this alarum and the noise?*
(*Henry VI part I 1.4*)

Albion NOUN Albion is another
word for England ❏ *but I will sell my
dukedom,/ To buy a slobbery and a
dirty farm In that nook-shotten isle of
Albion* (*Henry V 3.5*)

all of all PHRASE all of all means
everything, or the sum of all things
❏ *The very all of all* (*Love's Labours
Lost 5.1*)

amend VERB amend in this context
means to get better or to heal ❏ *at
his touch… They presently amend*
(*Macbeth 4.3*)

anchor VERB if you anchor on
something you concentrate on it or
fix on it ❏ *My invention ... Anchors
on Isabel* (*Measure for Measure 2.4*)

anon ADV anon was a common word
for soon ❏ *You shall see anon how the
murderer gets the love of Gonzago's
wife* (*Hamlet 3.2*)

antic 1 ADJ antic here means weird
or strange ❏ *I'll charm the air to give
a sound/ While you perform your antic
round* (*Macbeth 4.1*) 2 NOUN in
this context antic means a clown or
a strange, unattractive creature ❏ *If
black, why nature, drawing an antic,/
Made a foul blot* (*Much Ado About
Nothing 3.1*)

apace ADV apace was a common word
for quickly ❏ *Come apace* (*As You
Like It 3.3*)

apparel NOUN apparel means clothes or clothing ❑ *one suit of apparel* (*Hamlet 3.2*)

appliance NOUN appliance here means cure ❑ *Diseases desperate grown/ By desperate appliance are relieved* (*Hamlet 4.3*)

argument NOUN argument here means a topic of conversation or the subject ❑ *Why 'tis the rarest argument of wonder that hath shot out in our latter times* (*All's Well That Ends Well 2.3*)

arrant ADJ arrant means absolute, complete. It strengthens the meaning of a noun ❑ *Fortune, that arrant whore* (*King Lear 2.4*)

arras NOUN an arras is a tapestry, a large cloth with a picture sewn on it using coloured thread ❑ *Behind the arras I'll convey myself/ To hear the process* (*Hamlet 3.3*)

art 1 NOUN art in this context means knowledge ❑ *Their malady convinces/ The great essay of art* (*Macbeth 4.3*) 2 NOUN art can also mean skill as it does here ❑ *He ... gave you such a masterly report/ For art and exercise in your defence* (*Hamlet 4.7*) 3 NOUN art here means magic ❑ *Now I want/ Spirits to enforce, art to enchant* (*The Tempest 5 Epilogue*)

assay 1 NOUN an assay was an attempt, a try ❑ *Make assay./ Bow, stubborn knees* (*Hamlet 3.3*) 2 NOUN assay can also mean a test or a trial ❑ *he hath made assay of her virtue* (*Measure for Measure 3.1*)

attend (on/upon) VERB attend on means to wait for or to expect ❑ *Tarry I here, I but attend on death* (*Two Gentlemen of Verona 3.1*)

auditor NOUN an auditor was a member of an audience or someone who listens ❑ *I'll be an auditor* (*A Midsummer Night's Dream 3.1*)

aught NOUN aught was a common word which meant anything ❑ *if my love thou holdest at aught* (*Hamlet 4.3*)

aunt 1 NOUN an aunt was another word for an old woman and also means someone who talks a lot or a gossip ❑ *The wisest aunt telling the saddest tale* (*A Midsummer Night's Dream 2.1*) 2 NOUN aunt could also mean a mistress or a prostitute ❑ *the thrush and the jay/ Are summer songs for me and my aunts/ While we lie tumbling in the hay* (*The Winter's Tale 4.3*)

avaunt EXCLAM avaunt was a common word which meant go away ❑ *Avaunt, you curs!* (*King Lear 3.6*)

aye ADV here aye means always or ever ❑ *Whose state and honour I for aye allow* (*Richard II 5.2*)

baffle VERB baffle meant to be disgraced in public or humiliated ❑ *I am disgraced, impeached, and baffled here* (*Richard II 1.1*)

bald ADJ bald means trivial or silly ❑ *I knew 'twould be a bald conclusion* (*The Comedy of Errors 2.2*)

ban NOUN a ban was a curse or an evil spell ❑ *Sometimes with lunatic bans... Enforce their charity* (*King Lear 2.3*)

barren ADJ barren meant empty or hollow ❑ *now I let go your hand, I am barren.* (*Twelfth Night 1.3*)

base ADJ base is an adjective that means unworthy or dishonourable ❑ *civet is of a baser birth than tar* (*As You Like It 3.2*)

base 1 ADJ base can also mean of low social standing or someone who was not part of the ruling class ❑ *Why brand they us with 'base'? (King Lear 1.2)* 2 ADJ here base means poor quality ❑ *Base cousin,/ Darest thou break first? (Two Noble Kinsmen 3.3)*

bawdy NOUN bawdy means obscene or rude ❑ *Bloody, bawdy villain! (Hamlet 2.2)*

bear in hand PHRASE bear in hand means taken advantage of or fooled ❑ *This I made good to you In our last conference, passed in probation with you/How you were borne in hand (Macbeth 3.1)*

beard VERB to beard someone was to oppose or confront them ❑ *Com'st thou to beard me in Denmark? (Hamlet 2.2)*

beard, in one's PHRASE if you say something in someone's beard you say it to their face ❑ *I will verify as much in his beard (Henry V 3.2)*

beaver NOUN a beaver was a visor on a battle helmet ❑ *O yes, my lord, he wore his beaver up (Hamlet 1.2)*

become VERB if something becomes you it suits you or is appropriate to you ❑ *Nothing in his life became him like the leaving it (Macbeth 1.4)*

bed, brought to PHRASE to be brought to bed means to give birth ❑ *His wife but yesternight was brought to bed (Titus Andronicus 4.2)*

bedabbled ADJ if something is bedabbled it is sprinkled ❑ *Bedabbled with the dew, and torn with briers (A Midsummer Night's Dream 3.2)*

Bedlam NOUN Bedlam was a word used for Bethlehem Hospital which was a place the insane were sent to ❑ *The country give me proof and precedent/Of Bedlam beggars (King Lear 2.3)*

bed-swerver NOUN a bed-swerver was someone who was unfaithful in marriage, an adulterer ❑ *she's/A bed-swerver (Winter's Tale 2.1)*

befall 1 VERB to befall is to happen, occur or take place ❑ *In this same interlude it doth befall/That I present a wall (A Midsummer Night's Dream 5.1)* 2 VERB to befall can also mean to happen to someone or something ❑ *fair befall thee and thy noble house (Richard III 1.3)*

behoof NOUN behoof was an advantage or benefit ❑ *All our surgeons/Convent in their behoof (Two Noble Kinsmen 1.4)*

beldam NOUN a beldam was a witch or old woman ❑ *Have I not reason, beldams as you are? (Macbeth 3.5)*

belike ADV belike meant probably, perhaps or presumably ❑ *belike he likes it not (Hamlet 3.2)*

bent 1 NOUN bent means a preference or a direction ❑ *Let me work,/For I can give his humour true bent,/And I will bring him to the Capitol (Julius Caesar 2.1)* 2 ADJ if you are bent on something you are determined to do it ❑ *for now I am bent to know/By the worst means the worst. (Macbeth 3.4)*

beshrew VERB beshrew meant to curse or wish evil on someone ❑ *much beshrew my manners and my pride/If Hermia meant to say Lysander lied (A Midsummer Night's Dream 2.2)*

betime (s) ADV betime means early
   ❏ *To business that we love we rise
   betime* (*Antony and Cleopatra 4.4*)

bevy NOUN bevy meant type or sort,
   it was also used to mean company
   ❏ *many more of the same bevy*
   (*Hamlet 5.2*)

blazon VERB to blazon something
   meant to display or show it ❏ *that
   thy skill be more to blazon it* (*Romeo
   and Juliet 2.6*)

blind ADJ if you are blind when you
   do something you are reckless or
   do not care about the consequences
   ❏ *are you yet to your own souls so
   blind/ That two you will war with God
   by murdering me* (*Richard III 1.4*)

bombast NOUN bombast was wool
   stuffing (used in a cushion for
   example) and so it came to mean
   padded out or long-winded. Here it
   means someone who talks a lot about
   nothing in particular ❏ *How now my
   sweet creature of bombast* (*Henry IV
   part I 2.4*)

bond 1 NOUN a bond is a contract
   or legal deed ❏ *Well, then, your
   bond, and let me see* (*Merchant of
   Venice 1.3*) 2 NOUN bond could also
   mean duty or commitment
   ❏ *I love your majesty/ According to my
   bond* (*King Lear 1.1*)

bottom NOUN here bottom means
   essence, main point or intent ❏ *Now
   I see/ The bottom of your purpose*
   (*All's Well That Ends Well 3.7*)

bounteously ADV bounteously
   means plentifully, abundantly ❏ *I
   prithee, and I'll pay thee bounteously*
   (*Twelfth Night 1.2*)

brace 1 NOUN a brace is a couple or
   two ❏ *Have lost a brace of kinsmen*

(*Romeo and Juliet 5.3*) 2 NOUN if
   you are in a brace position it means
   you are ready ❏ *For that it stands not
   in such warlike brace* (*Othello 1.3*)

brand VERB to mark permanantly like
   the markings on cattle ❏ *the wheeled
   seat/ Of fortunate Caesar ... branded
   his baseness that ensued* (*Anthony
   and Cleopatra 4.14*)

brave ADJ brave meant fine, excellent
   or splendid ❏ *O brave new world/
   That has such people in't* (*The
   Tempest 5.1*)

brine NOUN brine is sea-water ❏ *He
   shall drink nought brine, for I'll not
   show him/ Where the quick freshes are*
   (*The Tempest 3.2*)

brow NOUN brow in this context
   means appearance ❏ *doth hourly
   grow/ Out of his brows* (*Hamlet 3.3*)

burden 1 NOUN the burden here
   is a chorus ❏ *I would sing my song
   without a burden* (*As You Like It 3.2*)
   2 NOUN burden means load or
   weight (this is the current meaning)
   ❏ *the scarfs and the bannerets about
   thee did manifoldly dissuade me
   from believing thee a vessel of too
   great a burden* (*All's Well that Ends
   Well 2.3*)

buttons, in one's PHRASE this is a
   phrase that means clear, easy to see
   ❏ *Tis in his buttons he will carry't*
   (*The Merry Wives of Windsor 3.2*)

cable NOUN cable here means scope
   or reach ❏ *The law ... Will give her
   cable* (*Othello 1.2*)

cadent ADJ if something is cadent it
   is falling or dropping ❏ *With cadent
   tears fret channels in her cheeks* (*King
   Lear 1.4*)

canker VERB to canker is to decay, become corrupt ❑ *And, as with age his body uglier grows,/ So his mind cankers* (*The Tempest 4.1*)

canon, from the PHRASE from the canon is an expression meaning out of order, improper ❑ *Twas from the canon* (*Coriolanus 3.1*)

cap-a-pie ADV cap-a-pie means from head to foot, completely ❑ *I am courtier cap-a-pie* (*The Winter's Tale 4.4*)

carbonadoed ADJ if something is carbonadoed it is cut or scored (scratched) with a knife ❑ *it is your carbonadoed* (*All's Well That Ends Well 4.5*)

carouse VERB to carouse is to drink at length, party ❑ *They cast their caps up and carouse together* (*Anthony and Cleopatra 4.12*)

carrack NOUN a carrack was a large old ship, a galleon ❑ *Faith, he tonight hath boarded a land-carrack* (*Othello 1.2*)

cassock NOUN a cassock here means a military cloak, long coat ❑ *half of the which dare not shake the snow from off their cassocks lest they shake themselves to pieces* (*All's Well That Ends Well 4.3*)

catastrophe NOUN catastrophe here means conclusion or end ❑ *pat he comes, like the catastrophe of the old comedy* (*King Lear 1.2*)

cautel NOUN a cautel was a trick or a deceptive act ❑ *Perhaps he loves you now/ And now no soil not cautel doth besmirch* (*Hamlet 1.2*)

celerity NOUN celerity was a common word for speed, swiftness ❑ *Hence hath offence his quick celerity/ When it is borne in high authority* (*Measure for Measure 4.2*)

chafe NOUN chafe meant anger or temper ❑ *this Herculean Roman does become/ The carriage of his chafe* (*Anthony and Cleopatra 1.3*)

chanson NOUN chanson was an old word for a song ❑ *The first row of the pious chanson will show you more* (*Hamlet 2.2*)

chapman NOUN a chapman was a trader or merchant ❑ *Not uttered by base sale of chapman's tongues* (*Love's Labours Lost 2.1*)

chaps, chops NOUN chaps (and chops) was a word for jaws ❑ *Which ne'er shook hands nor bade farewell to him/ Till he unseamed him from the nave to th' chops* (*Macbeth 1.2*)

chattels NOUN chattels were your moveable possessions. The word is used in the traditional marriage ceremony ❑ *She is my goods, my chattels* (*The Taming of the Shrew 3.3*)

chide VERB if you are chided by someone you are told off or reprimanded ❑ *Now I but chide, but I should use thee worse* (*A Midsummer Night's Dream 3.2*)

chinks NOUN chinks was a word for cash or money ❑ *he that can lay hold of her/ Shall have the chinks* (*Romeo and Juliet 1.5*)

choleric ADJ if something was called choleric it meant that they were quick to get angry ❑ *therewithal unruly waywardness that infirm and choleric years bring with them* (*King Lear 1.1*)

chuff NOUN a chuff was a miser,

someone who clings to his or her money ❑ *ye fat chuffs* (*Henry IV part I 2.2*)

cipher NOUN cipher here means nothing ❑ *Mine were the very cipher of a function* (*Measure for Measure 2.2*)

circummured ADJ circummured means that something is surrounded with a wall ❑ *He hath a garden circummured with brick* (*Measure for Measure 4.1*)

civet NOUN a civet is a type of scent or perfume ❑ *Give me an ounce of civet* (*King Lear 4.6*)

clamorous ADJ clamorous means noisy or boisterous ❑ *Be clamorous and leap all civil bounds* (*Twelfth Night 1.4*)

clangour, clangor NOUN clangour is a word that means ringing (the sound that bells make) ❑ *Like to a dismal clangour heard from far* (*Henry VI part III 2.3*)

cleave VERB if you cleave to something you stick to it or are faithful to it ❑ *Thy thoughts I cleave to* (*The Tempest 4.1*)

clock and clock, 'twixt PHRASE from hour to hour, without stopping or continuously ❑ *To weep 'twixt clock and clock* (*Cymbeline 3.4*)

close ADJ here close means hidden ❑ *Stand close; this is the same Athenian* (*A Midsummer Night's Dream 3.2*)

cloud NOUN a cloud on your face means that you have a troubled, unhappy expression ❑ *He has cloud in's face* (*Anthony and Cleopatra 3.2*)

cloy VERB if you cloy an appetite you satisfy it ❑ *Other women cloy/The*

appetites they feed (*Anthony and Cleopatra 2.2*)

cock-a-hoop, set PHRASE if you set cock-a-hoop you become free of everything ❑ *You will set cock-a-hoop* (*Romeo and Juliet 1.5*)

colours NOUN colours is a word used to describe battle-flags or banners. Sometimes we still say that we nail our colours to the mast if we are stating which team or side of an argument we support ❑ *the approbation of those that weep this lamentable divorce under her colours* (*Cymbeline 1.5*)

combustion NOUN combustion was a word meaning disorder or chaos ❑ *prophesying ... Of dire combustion and confused events* (*Macbeth 2.3*)

comely ADJ if you are or something is comely you or it is lovely, beautiful, graceful ❑ *O, what a world is this, when what is comely/Envenoms him that bears it!* (*As You Like It 2.3*)

commend VERB if you commend yourself to someone you send greetings to them ❑ *Commend me to my brother* (*Measure for Measure 1.4*)

compact NOUN a compact is an agreement or a contract ❑ *what compact mean you to have with us?* (*Julius Caesar 3.1*)

compass 1 NOUN here compass means range or scope ❑ *you would sound me from my lowest note to the top of my compass* (*Hamlet 3.2*) 2 VERB to compass here means to achieve, bring about or make happen ❑ *How now shall this be compassed?/ Canst thou bring me to the party?* (*Tempest 3.2*)

comptible ADJ comptible is an old word meaning sensitive ❑ *I am very comptible, even to the least sinister usage.* (*Twelfth Night 1.5*)

confederacy NOUN a confederacy is a group of people usually joined together to commit a crime. It is another word for a conspiracy ❑ *Lo, she is one of this confederacy!* (*A Midsummer Night's Dream 3.2*)

confound VERB if you confound something you confuse it or mix it up; it also means to stop or prevent ❑ *A million fail, confounding oath on oath.* (*A Midsummer Night's Dream 3.2*)

contagion NOUN contagion is an old word for disease or poison ❑ *hell itself breathes out/Contagion to this world* (*Hamlet 3.2*)

contumely NOUN contumely is an old word for an insult ❑ *the proud man's contumely* (*Hamlet 3.1*)

counterfeit 1 VERB if you counterfeit something you copy or imitate it ❑ *Meantime your cheeks do counterfeit our roses* (*Henry VI part I 2.4*) 2 VERB in this context counterfeit means to pretend or make believe ❑ *I will counterfeit the bewitchment of some popular man* (*Coriolanus*)

coz NOUN coz was a shortened form of the word cousin ❑ *sweet my coz, be merry* (*As You Like It 1.2*)

cozenage NOUN cozenage is an old word meaning cheating or a deception ❑ *Thrown out his angle for my proper life,/And with such coz'nage* (*Hamlet 5.2*)

crave VERB crave used to mean to beg or request ❑ *I crave your pardon* (*The Comedy of Errors 1.2*)

crotchet NOUN crotchets are strange ideas or whims ❑ *thou hast some strange crotchets in thy head now* (*The Merry Wives of Windsor 2.1*)

cuckold NOUN a cuckold is a man whose wife has been unfaithful to him ❑ *As there is no true cuckold but calamity* (*Twelfth Night 1.5*)

cuffs, go to PHRASE this phrase meant to fight ❑ *the player went to cuffs in the question* (*Hamlet 2.2*)

cup VERB in this context cup is a verb which means to pour drink or fill glasses with alcohol ❑ *cup us til the world go round* (*Anthony and Cleopatra 2.7*)

cur NOUN cur is an insult meaning dog and is also used to mean coward ❑ *Out, dog! out, cur! Thou drivest me past the bounds/Of maiden's patience* (*A Midsummer Night's Dream 3.2*)

curiously ADV in this context curiously means carefully or skilfully ❑ *The sleeves curiously cut* (*The Taming of the Shrew 4.3*)

curry VERB curry means to flatter or to praise someone more than they are worth ❑ *I would curry with Master Shallow that no man could better command his servants* (*Henry IV part II 5.1*)

custom NOUN custom is a habit or a usual practice ❑ *Hath not old custom made this life more sweet/Than that of painted pomp?* (*As You Like It 2.1*)

cutpurse NOUN a cutpurse is an old word for a thief. Men used to carry their money in small bags (purse) that hung from their belts; thieves would cut the purse from the belt and steal their money ❑ *A cutpurse of the empire and the rule* (*Hamlet 3.4*)

dainty ADJ dainty used to mean splendid, fine ❏ *Why, that's my dainty Ariel!* (*Tempest 5.1*)

dally VERB if you dally with something you play with it or tease it ❏ *They that dally nicely with words may quickly make them wanton* (*Twelfth Night 3.1*)

damask COLOUR damask is a light-red or pink colour ❏ *Twas just the difference/Betwixt the constant red and mingled damask* (*As You Like It 3.5*)

dare 1 VERB dare means to challeng or, confront ❏ *He goes before me, and still dares me on* (*A Midsummer Night's Dream 3.3*) 2 VERB dare in this context means to present, deliver or inflict ❏ *all that fortune, death, and danger dare* (*Hamlet 4.4*)

darkly ADV darkly was used in this context to mean secretly or cunningly ❏ *I will go darkly to work with her* (*Measure for Measure 5.1*)

daw NOUN a daw was a slang term for idiot or fool (after the bird jackdaw which was famous for its stupidity) ❏ *Yea, just so much as you may take upon a knife's point and choke a daw withal* (*Much Ado About Nothing 3.1*)

debile ADJ debile meant weak or feeble ❏ *And debile minister great power* (*All's Well That Ends Well 2.3*)

deboshed ADJ deboshed was another way of saying corrupted or debauched ❏ *Men so disordered, deboshed and bold* (*King Lear 1.4*)

decoct VERB to decoct was to heat up, warm something ❏ *Can sodden water,/A drench for sur-reained jades* *... Decoct their cold blood to such valiant heat?* (*Henry V 3.5*)

deep-revolving ADJ deep-revolving here uses the idea that you turn something over in your mind when you are thinking hard about it and so means deep-thinking, meditating ❏ *The deep-revolving Buckingham/No more shall be the neighbour to my counsels* (*Richard III 4.2*)

defect NOUN defect here means shortcoming or something that is not right ❏ *Being unprepared/Our will became the servant to defect* (*Macbeth 2.1*)

degree 1 NOUN degree here means rank, standing or station ❏ *Should a like language use to all degrees,/And mannerly distinguishment leave out/Betwixt the prince and beggar* (*The Winter's Tale 2.1*) 2 NOUN in this context, degree means extent or measure ❏ *her offence/Must be of such unnatural degree* (*King Lear 1.1*)

deify VERB if you deify something or someone you worship it or them as a God ❏ *all.. deifying the name of Rosalind* (*As You Like It 3.2*)

delated ADJ delated here means detailed ❏ *the scope/Of these delated articles* (*Hamlet 1.2*)

delicate ADJ if something was described as delicate it meant it was of fine quality or valuable ❏ *thou wast a spirit too delicate* (*The Tempest 1.2*)

demise VERB in this context demise means to transmit, give or convey ❏ *what state ... Canst thou demise to any child of mine?* (*Richard III 4.4*)

deplore VERB to deplore means to express with grief or sorrow ❏ *Never more/ Will I my master's tears to you deplore* (*Twelfth Night 3.1*)

depose VERB if you depose someone you make them take an oath, or swear something to be true ❏ *Depose him in the justice of his cause* (*Richard II 1.3*)

depositary NOUN a depositary is a trustee ❏ *Made you … my depositary* (*King Lear 2.4*)

derive 1 VERB to derive means to comes from or to descend (it usually applies to people) ❏ *No part of it is mine,/ This shame derives itself from unknown loins.* (*Much Ado About Nothing 4.1*) 2 VERB if you derive something from someone you inherit it ❏ *Treason is not inherited …Or, if we derive it from our friends/ What's that to me?* (*As You Like It 1.3*)

descry VERB to see or catch sight of ❏ *The news is true, my lord. He is descried* (*Anthony and Cleopatra 3.7*)

desert 1 NOUN desert means worth or merit ❏ *That dost in vile misproson shackle up/ My love and her desert* (*All's Well That Ends Well 2.3*) 2 ADJ desert is used here to mean lonely or isolated ❏ *if that love or gold/ Can in this desert place buy entertainment* (*As You LIke It 2.4*)

design 1 VERB to design means to indicate or point out ❏ *we shall see/ Justice design the victor's chivalry* (*Richard II 1.1*) 2 NOUN a design is a plan, an intention or an undertaking ❏ *hinder not the honour of his design* (*All's Well That Ends Well 3.6*)

designment NOUN a designment was a plan or undertaking ❏ *The desperate tempest hath so bang'd the Turks,/ That their designment halts* (*Othello 2.1*)

despite VERB despite here means to spite or attempt to thwart a plan ❏ *Only to despite them I will endeavour anything* (*Much Ado About Nothing 2.2*)

device NOUN a device is a plan, plot or trick ❏ *Excellent, I smell a device* (*Twelfth Night 2.3*)

disable VERB to disable here means to devalue or make little of ❏ *he disabled my judgement* (*As You Like It 5.4*)

discandy VERB here discandy means to melt away or dissolve ❏ *The hearts … do discandy , melt their sweets* (*Anthony and Cleopatra 4.12*)

disciple VERB to disciple is to teach or train ❏ *He …was/ Discipled of the bravest* (*All's Well That Ends Well 1.2*)

discommend VERB if you discommend something you criticize it ❏ *my dialect which you discommend so much* (*King Lear 2.2*)

discourse NOUN discourse means conversation, talk or chat ❏ *which part of it I'll waste/ With such discourse as I not doubt shall make it/ Go quick away* (*The Tempest 5.1*)

discover VERB discover used to mean to reveal or show ❏ *the Prince discovered to Claudio that he loved my niece* (*Much Ado About Nothing 1.2*)

disliken VERB disguise, make unlike ❏ *disliken/ The truth of your own seeming* (*The Winter's Tale 4.4*)

dismantle VERB to dismantle is to remove or take away ❏ *Commit a thing so monstrous to dismantle/*

So many folds of favour (*King Lear 1.1*)

disponge VERB disponge means to pour out or rain down ❏ *The poisonous damp of night disponge upon me* (*Anthony and Cleopatra 4.9*)

distrain VERB to distrain something is to confiscate it ❏ *My father's goods are all distrained and sold* (*Richard II 2.3*)

divers ADJ divers is an old word for various ❏ *I will give out divers schedules of my beauty* (*Twelfth Night 1.5*)

doff VERB to doff is to get rid of or dispose ❏ *make our women fight/ To doff their dire distresses* (*Macbeth 4.3*)

dog VERB if you dog someone or something you follow them or it closely ❏ *I will rather leave to see Hector than not to dog him* (*Troilus and Cressida 5.1*)

dotage NOUN dotage here means infatuation ❏ *Her dotage now I do begin to pity* (*A Midsummer Night's Dream 4.1*)

dotard NOUN a dotard was an old fool ❏ *I speak not like a dotard nor a fool* (*Much Ado About Nothing 5.1*)

dote VERB to dote is to love, cherish, care without seeing any fault ❏ *And won her soul; and she, sweet lady, dotes,/ Devoutly dotes, dotes in idolatry* (*A Midsummer Night's Dream 1.1*)

doublet NOUN a doublet was a man's close-fitting jacket with short skirt ❏ *Lord Hamlet, with his doublet all unbraced* (*Hamlet 2.1*)

dowager NOUN a dowager is a widow ❏ *Like to a step-dame or a dowage* (*A Midsummer Night's Dream 1.1*)

dowdy NOUN a dowdy was an ugly woman ❏ *Dido was a dowdy* (*Romeo and Juliet 2.4*)

dower NOUN a dower (or dowery) is the riches or property given by the father of a bride to her husband-to-be ❏ *Thy truth then by they dower* (*King Lear 1.1*)

dram NOUN a dram is a tiny amount ❏ *Why, everything adheres together that no dram of a scruple* (*Twelfth Night 3.4*)

drift NOUN drift is a plan, scheme or intention ❏ *Shall Romeo by my letters know our drift* (*Romeo and Juliet 4.1*)

dropsied ADJ dropsied means pretentious ❏ *Where great additions swell's and virtues none/ It is a dropsied honour* (*All's Well That Ends Well 2.3*)

drudge NOUN a drudge was a slave, servant ❏ *If I be his cuckold, he's my drudge* (*All's Well That Ends Well 1.3*)

dwell VERB to dwell sometimes meant to exist, to be ❏ *I'd rather dwell in my necessity* (*Merchant of Venice 1.3*)

earnest ADJ an earnest was a pledge to pay or a payment in advance ❏ *for an earnest of a greater honour/ He bade me from him call thee Thane of Cawdor* (*Macbeth 1.3*)

ecstasy NOUN madness ❏ *This is the very ecstasy of love* (*Hamlet 2.1*)

edict NOUN law or declaration ❏ *It stands as an edict in destiny.* (*A Midsummer Night's Dream 1.1*)

egall ADJ egall is an old word meaning equal ❏ *companions/Whose souls do bear an egall yoke of love* (Merchant of Venice 2.4)

eisel NOUN eisel meant vinegar ❏ *Woo't drink up eisel?* (Hamlet 5.1)

eke, eke out VERB eke meant to add to, to increase. Eke out nowadays means to make something last as long as possible – particularly in the sense of making money last a long time ❏ *Still be kind/And eke out our performance with your mind* (Henry V Chorus)

elbow, out at PHRASE out at elbow is an old phrase meaning in poor condition – as when your jacket sleeves are worn at the elbow which shows that it is an old jacket ❏ *He cannot, sir. He's out at elbow* (Measure for Measure 2.1)

element NOUN elements were thought to be the things from which all things were made. They were: air, earth, water and fire ❏ *Does not our lives consist of the four elements?* (Twelfth Night 2.3)

elf VERB to elf was to tangle ❏ *I'll ... elf all my hairs in knots* (King Lear 2.3)

embassy NOUN an embassy was a message ❏ *We'll once more hear Orsino's embassy.* (Twelfth Night 1.5)

emphasis NOUN emphasis here means a forceful expression or strong statement ❏ *What is he whose grief/Bears such an emphasis* (Hamlet 5.1)

empiric NOUN an empiric was an untrained doctor sometimes called a quack ❏ *we must not ... prostitute our past-cure malady/To empirics* (All's Well That Ends Well 2.1)

emulate ADJ emulate here means envious ❏ *pricked on by a most emulate pride* (Hamlet 1.1)

enchant VERB to enchant meant to put a magic spell on ❏ *Damn'd as thou art, thou hast enchanted her,/For I'll refer me to all things of sense* (Othello 1.2)

enclog VERB to enclog was to hinder something or to provide an obstacle to it ❏ *Traitors enscarped to enclog the guitless keel* (Othello 1.2)

endure VERB to endure was to allow or to permit ❏ *and will endure/Our setting down before't.* (Macbeth 5.4)

enfranchise VERB if you enfranchised something you set it free ❏ *Do this or this;/Take in that kingdom and enfranchise that;/Perform't, or else we damn thee.'* (Anthony and Cleopatra 1.1)

engage VERB to engage here means to pledge or to promise ❏ *This to be true I do engage my life* (As You Like It 5.4)

engaol VERB to lock up or put in prison ❏ *Within my mouth you have engaoled my tongue* (Richard II 1.3)

engine NOUN an engine was a plot, device or a machine ❏ *their promises, enticements, oaths, tokens, and all these engines, of lust, are not the things they go under* (All's Well That Ends Well 3.5)

englut VERB if you were engulfed you were swallowed up or eaten whole ❏ *For certainly thou art so near the gulf,/Thou needs must be englutted.* (Henry V 4.3)

enjoined ADJ enjoined describes people joined together for the same reason ❏ *Of enjoined penitents/*

There's four or five (*All's Well That Ends Well* 3.5)

entertain 1 VERB to entertain here means to welcome or receive ❑ *Approach, rich Ceres, her to entertain.* (*The Tempest* 4.1) 2 VERB to entertain in this context means to cherish, hold in high regard or to respect ❑ *and I quake,/ Lest thou a feverous life shouldst entertain/ And six or seven winters more respect/ Than a perpetual honour.* (*Measure for Measure* 3.1) 3 VERB to entertain means here to give something consideration ❑ *But entertain it,/ And though you think me poor, I am the man/ Will give thee all the world.* (*Anthony and Cleopatra* 2.7) 4 VERB to entertain here means to treat or handle ❑ *your highness is not entertained with that ceremonious affection as you were wont* (*King Lear* 1.4)

envious ADJ envious meant spiteful or vindictive ❑ *he shall appear to the envious a scholar* (*Measure for Measure* 3.2)

ere PREP ere was a common word for before ❑ *ere this I should ha' fatted all the region kites* (*Hamlet* 2.2)

err VERB to err means to go astray, to make a mistake ❑ *And as he errs, doting on Hermia's eyes* (*A Midsummer Night's Dream* 1.1)

erst ADV erst was a common word for once or before ❑ *that erst brought sweetly forth/ The freckled cowslip* (*Henry V* 5.2)

eschew VERB if you eschew something you deliberately avoid doing it ❑ *What cannot be eschewed must be embraced* (*The Merry Wives of Windsor* 5.5)

escote VERB to escote meant to pay for, support ❑ *How are they escoted?* (*Hamlet* 2.2)

estimable ADJ estimable meant appreciative ❑ *I could not with such estimable wonder over-far believe that* (*Twelfth Night* 2.1)

extenuate VERB extenuate means to lessen ❑ *Which by no means we may extenuate* (*A Midsummer Night's Dream* 1.1)

fain ADV fain was a common word meaning gladly or willingly ❑ *I would fain prove so* (*Hamlet* 2.2)

fall NOUN in a voice or music fall meant going higher and lower ❑ *and so die/ That strain again! it had a dying fall* (*Twelfth Night* 1.1)

false ADJ false was a common word for treacherous ❑ *this is counter, you false Danish dogs!* (*Hamlet* 4.5)

fare VERB fare means to get on or manage ❑ *I fare well* (*The Taming of the Shrew Introduction* 2)

feign VERB to feign was to make up, pretend or fake ❑ *It is the more like to be feigned* (*Twelfth Night* 1.5)

fie EXCLAM fie was an exclamation of disgust ❑ *Fie, that you'll say so!* (*Twelfth Night* 1.3)

figure VERB to figure was to symbolize or look like ❑ *Wings and no eyes, figure unheedy haste* (*A Midsummer Night's Dream* 1.1)

filch VERB if you filch something you steal it ❑ *With cunning hast thou filch'd my daughter's heart* (*A Midsummer Night's Dream* 1.1)

flout VERB to flout something meant to scorn it ❑ *Why will you suffer her to flout me thus?* (*A Midsummer Night's Dream* 3.2)

fond ADJ fond was a common word meaning foolish ❑ *Shall we their fond pageant see?* (*A Midsummer Night's Dream 3.2*)

footing 1 NOUN footing meant landing on shore, arrival, disembarkation ❑ *Whose footing here anticipates our thoughts/A se'nnight's speed.* (*Othello 2.1*) 2 NOUN footing also means support ❑ *there your charity would have lacked footing* (*Winter's Tale 3.3*)

forsooth ADV in truth, certainly, truly
❑ *I had rather, forsooth, go before you like a man* (*The Merry Wives of Windsor 3.2*)

forswear VERB if you forswear you lie, swear falsely or break your word ❑ *he swore a thing to me on Monday night, which he forswore on Tuesday morning* (*Much Ado About Nothing 5.1*)

freshes NOUN a fresh is a fresh water stream ❑ *He shall drink nought brine, for I'll not show him/Where the quick freshes are.* (*Tempest 3.2*)

furlong NOUN a furlong is a measure of distance. It is the equivalent on one eight of a mile ❑ *Now would I give a thousand furlongs of sea for an acre of barren ground* (*Tempest 1.1*)

gaberdine NOUN a gaberdine is a cloak ❑ *My best way is to creep under his gaberdine* (*Tempest 2.2*)

gage NOUN a gage was a challenge to duel or fight ❑ *There is my gage, Aumerle, in gage to thine* (*Richard II 4.1*)

gait NOUN your gait is your way of walking or step ❑ *I know her by her gait* (*Tempest 4.1*)

gall VERB to gall is to annoy or irritate ❑ *Let it not gall your patience, good Iago,/That I extend my manners* (*Othello 2.1*)

gambol NOUN frolic or play ❑ *Hop in his walks, and gambol in his eyes* (*A Midsummer Night's Dream 3.1*)

gaskins NOUN gaskins is an old word for trousers ❑ *or, if both break, your gaskins fall.* (*Twelfth Night 1.5*)

gentle ADJ gentle means noble or well-born ❑ *thrice-gentle Cassio!* (*Othello 3.4*)

glass NOUN a glass was another word for a mirror ❑ *no woman's face remember/Save from my glass, mine own* (*Tempest 3.1*)

gleek VERB to gleek means to make a joke or jibe ❑ *Nay, I can gleek upon occasion* (*A Midsummer Night's Dream 3.1*)

gust NOUN gust meant taste, desire or enjoyment. We still say that if you do something with gusto you do it with enjoyment or enthusiasm ❑ *the gust he hath in quarrelling* (*Twelfth Night 1.3*)

habit NOUN habit means clothes ❑ *You know me by my habit* (*Henry V 3.6*)

heaviness NOUN heaviness means sadness or grief ❑ *So sorrow's heaviness doth heavier grow/For debt that bankrupt sleep doth sorrow owe* (*A Midsummer Night's Dream 3.2*)

heavy ADJ if you are heavy you are said to be sad or sorrowful ❑ *Away from light steals home my heavy son* (*Romeo and Juliet 1.1*)

hie VERB to hie meant to hurry ❑ *My husband hies him home* (*All Well That Ends Well 4.4*)

hollowly ADV if you did something hollowly you did it insincerely ❑ *If hollowly invert/ What best is boded me to mischief!* (*Tempest 3.1*)

holy-water, court PHRASE if you court holy water you make empty promises, or make statements which sound good but have no real meaning ❑ *court holy-water in a dry house is better than this rain-water out o'door* (*King Lear 3.2*)

howsoever ADV howsoever was often used instead of however ❑ *But howsoever strange and admirable* (*A Midsummer Night's Dream 5.1*)

humour NOUN your humour was your mood, frame of mind or temperament ❑ *it fits my humour well* (*As You Like It 3.2*)

ill ADJ ill means bad ❑ *I must thank him only,/ Let my remembrance suffer ill report* (*Antony and Cleopatra 2.2*)

indistinct ADJ inseparable or unable to see a difference ❑ *Even till we make the main and the aerial blue/ An indistinct regard.* (*Othello 2.1*)

indulgence NOUN indulgence meant approval ❑ *As you from crimes would pardoned be,/ Let your indulgence set me free* (*The Tempest Epilogue*)

infirmity NOUN infirmity was weakness or fraility ❑ *Be not disturbed with my infirmity* (*The Tempest 4.1*)

intelligence NOUN here intelligence means information ❑ *Pursue her; and for this intelligence/ If I have thanks* (*A Midsummer Night's Dream 1.1*)

inwards NOUN inwards meant someone's internal organs ❑ *the thought whereof/ Doth like a poisonous mineral gnaw my inwards* (*Othello 2.1*)

issue 1 NOUN the issue of a marriage are the children ❑ *To thine and Albany's issues,/ Be this perpetual* (*King Lear 1.1*) 2 NOUN in this context issue means outcome or result ❑ *I am to pray you, not to strain my speech,/ To grosser issues* (*Othello*)

kind NOUN kind here means situation or case ❑ *But in this kind, wanting your father's voice,/ The other must be held the worthier.* (*A Midsummer Night's Dream 1.1*)

knave NOUN a knave was a common word for scoundrel ❑ *How absolute the knave is!* (*Hamlet 5.1*)

league NOUN A distance. A league was the distance a person could walk in one hour ❑ *From Athens is her house remote seven leagues* (*A Midsummer Night's Dream 1.1*)

lief, had as ADJ I had as lief means I should like just as much ❑ *I had as lief the town crier spoke my lines* (*Hamlet 1.2*)

livery NOUN livery was a costume, outfit, uniform usually worn by a servant ❑ *You can endure the livery of a nun* (*A Midsummer Night's Dream 1.1*)

loam NOUN loam is soil containing decayed vegetable matter and therefore good for growing crops and plants ❑ *and let him have some plaster, or some loam, or some rough-cast about him, to signify wall* (*A Midsummer Night's Dream 3.1*)

lusty ADJ lusty meant strong ❑ *and oared/ Himself with his good arms in lusty stroke/ To th' shore* (*The Tempest 2.1*)

maidenhead NOUN maidenhead means chastity or virginity ❑ *What I am, and what I would, are as secret as maidenhead* (*Twelfth Night 1.5*)

mark VERB mark means to note or pay attention to ❑ *Where sighs and groans,/ Are made not marked* (*Macbeth 4.3*)

marvellous ADJ very or extremely ❑ *here's a marvellous convenient place for our rehearsal* (*A Midsummer Night's Dream 3.1*)

meet ADJ right or proper ❑ *tis most meet you should* (*Macbeth 5.1*)

merely ADV completely or entirely ❑ *Love is merely a madness* (*As You Like It 3.2*)

misgraffed ADJ misgraffed is an old word for mismatched or unequal ❑ *Or else misgraffed in respect of years* (*A Midsummer Night's Dream 1.1*)

misprision NOUN a misprision meant an error or mistake ❑ *Misprision in the highest degree!* (*Twelfth Night 1.5*)

mollification NOUN mollification is appeasement or a way of preventing someone getting angry ❑ *I am to hull here a little longer. Some mollification for your giant* (*Twelfth Night 1.5*)

mouth, cold in the PHRASE a well-known saying of the time which meant to be dead ❑ *What, must our mouths be cold?* (*The Tempest 1.1*)

murmur NOUN murmur was another word for rumour or hearsay ❑ *and then 'twas fresh in murmur* (*Twelfth Night 1.2*)

murrain NOUN murrain was another word for plague, pestilence ❑ *A murrain on your monster, and the devil take your fingers!* (*The Tempest 3.2*)

neaf NOUN neaf meant fist ❑ *Give me your neaf, Monsieur Mustardseed* (*A Midsummer Night's Dream 4.1*)

nice 1 ADJ nice had a number of meanings here it means fussy or particular ❑ *An therefore, goaded with most sharp occasions,/ Which lay nice manners by, I put you to/ The use of your own virtues* (*All's Well That Ends Well 5.1*) 2 ADJ nice here means critical or delicate ❑ *We're good… To set so rich a man/ On the nice hazard of one doubtful hour?* (*Henry IV part 1*) 3 ADJ nice in this context means carefully accurate, fastidious ❑ *O relation/ Too nice and yet too true!* (*Macbeth 4.3*) 4 ADJ trivial, unimportant ❑ *Romeo .. Bid him bethink/ How nice the quarrel was* (*Romeo and Juliet 3.1*)

nonpareil NOUN if you are nonpareil you are without equal, peerless ❑ *though you were crown'd/ The nonpareil of beauty!* (*Twelfth Night 1.5*)

office NOUN office here means business or work ❑ *Speak your office* (*Twelfth Night 1.5*)

outsport VERB outsport meant to overdo ❑ *Let's teach ourselves that honorable stop,/ Not to outsport discretion.* (*Othello 2.2*)

owe VERB owe meant own, possess ❑ *Lend less than thou owest* (*King Lear 1.4*)

paragon 1 VERB to paragon was to surpass or excede ❑ *he hath achieved a maid/ That paragons description and wild fame* (*Othello 2.1*) 2 VERB to paragon could also mean to compare with ❑ *I will give thee* bloody teeth *If thou with Caesar paragon again/ My man of men* (*Anthony and Cleopatra 1.5*)

pate NOUN pate is another word for head ❑ *Back, slave, or I will break thy pate across* (*The Comedy of Errors 2.1*)

paunch VERB to paunch someone is to stab (usually in the stomach). Paunch is still a common word for a stomach ❑ *Batter his skull, or paunch him with a stake* (*The Tempest 3.2*)

peevish ADJ if you are peevish you are irritable or easily angered ❑ *Run after that same peevish messenger* (*Twelfth Night 1.5*)

peradventure ADV perhaps or maybe ❑ *Peradventure this is not Fortune's work* (*As You Like It 1.2*)

perforce 1 ADV by force or violently ❑ *my rights and royalties,/ Plucked from my arms perforce* (*Richard II 2.3*) 2 ADV necessarily ❑ *The hearts of men, they must perforce have melted* (*Richard II 5.2*)

personage NOUN personage meant your appearance ❑ *Of what personage and years is he?* (*Twelfth Night 1.5*)

pestilence NOUN pestilence was a common word for plague or disease ❑ *Methought she purg'd the air of pestilence!* (*Twelfth Night 1.1*)

physic NOUN physic was medicine or a treatment ❑ *tis a physic/ That's bitter to sweet end* (*Measure for Measure 4.6*)

place NOUN place means a person's position or rank ❑ *Sons, kinsmen, thanes,/ And you whose places are the nearest* (*Macbeth 1.4*)

post NOUN here a post means a messenger ❑ *there are twenty weak and wearied posts/ Come from the north* (*Henry IV part II 2.4*)

pox NOUN pox was a word for any disease during which the victim had blisters on the skin. It was also a curse, a swear word ❑ *The pox of such antic, lisping, affecting phantasims* (*Romeo and Juliet 2.4*)

prate VERB to prate means to chatter ❑ *if thou prate of mountains* (*Hamlet 5.1*)

prattle VERB to prattle is to chatter or talk without purpose ❑ *I prattle out of fashion, and I dote In mine own comforts* (*Othello 2.1*)

precept NOUN a precept was an order or command ❑ *and my father's precepts I therein do forget.* (*The Tempest 3.1*)

present ADJ present here means immediate ❑ *We'll put the matter to the present push* (*Hamlet 5.1*)

prithee EXCLAM prithee is the equivalent of please or may I ask – a polite request ❑ *I prithee, and I'll pay thee bounteously* (*Twelfth Night 1.2*)

prodigal NOUN a prodigal is someone who wastes or squanders money ❑ *he's a very fool, and a prodigal* (*Twelfth Night 1.3*)

purpose NOUN purpose is used here to mean intention ❑ *understand my purposes aright* (*King Lear 1.4*)

quaff VERB quaff was a common word which meant to drink heavily or take a big drink ❑ *That quaffing and drinking will undo you* (*Twelfth Night 1.3*)

quaint 1 ADJ clever, ingenious ❑ *with a quaint device* (*The Tempest 3.3*) 2 ADJ cunning ❑ *I'll... tell quaint lies* (*Merchant of Venice 3.4*) 3 ADJ pretty, attractive ❑ *The clamorous owl, that nightly hoots and wonders/At our quaint spirit* (*A Midsummer Night's Dream 2.2*)

quoth VERB an old word which means say ❑ *'Tis dinner time.' quoth I* (*The Comedy of Errors 2.1*)

rack NOUN a rack described clouds or a cloud formation ❑ *And, like this insubstantial pageant faded,/ Leave not a rack behind* (*The Tempest 4.1*)

rail VERB to rant or swear at. It is still used occasionally today ❑ *Why do I rail on thee* (*Richard II 5.5*)

rate NOUN rate meant estimate, opinion ❑ *My son is lost, and, in my rate, she too* (*The Tempest 2.1*)

recreant NOUN recreant is an old word which means coward ❑ *Come, recreant, come, thou child* (*A Midsummer Night's Dream 3.2*)

remembrance NOUN remembrance is used here to mean memory or recollection ❑ *our remembrances of days foregone* (*All's Well That Ends Well 1.3*)

resolute ADJ firm or not going to change your mind ❑ *You are resolute, then?* (*Twelfth Night 1.5*)

revels NOUN revels means celebrations or a party ❑ *Our revels now are ended* (*The Tempest 4.1*)

rough-cast NOUN a mixture of lime and gravel (sometimes shells too) for use on an outer wall ❑ *and let him have some plaster, or some loam, or some rough-cast about him, to signify wall* (*A Midsummer Night's Dream 3.1*)

sack NOUN sack was another word for wine ❑ *My man-monster hath drowned his tongue in sack.* (*The Tempest 3.2*)

sad ADJ in this context sad means serious, grave ❑ *comes me the Prince and Claudio... in sad conference* (*Much Ado About Nothing 1.3*)

sampler NOUN a piece of embroidery, which often showed the family tree ❑ *Both on one sampler, sitting on one cushion* (*A Midsummer Night's Dream 3.2*)

saucy ADJ saucy means rude ❑ *I heard you were saucy at my gates* (*Twelfth Night 1.5*)

schooling NOUN schooling means advice ❑ *I have some private schooling for you both.* (*A Midsummer Night's Dream 1.1*)

seething ADJ seething in this case means boiling – we now use seething when we are very angry ❑ *Lovers and madmen have such seething brains* (*A Midsummer Night's Dream 5.1*)

semblative ADJ semblative means resembling or looking like ❑ *And all is semblative a woman's part.* (*Twelfth Night 1.4*)

several ADJ several here means separate or different ❑ *twenty several messengers* (*Anthony and Cleopatra 1.5*)

shrew NOUN An annoying person or someone who makes you cross ❑ *Bless you, fair shrew.* (*Twelfth Night 1.3*)

shroud VERB to shroud is to hide or shelter ❏ *I will here, shroud till the dregs of the storm be past* (*The Tempest 2.2*)

sickleman NOUN a sickleman was someone who used a sickle to harvest crops ❏ *You sunburnt sicklemen, of August weary* (*The Tempest 4.1*)

soft ADV soft here means wait a moment or stop ❏ *But, soft, what nymphs are these* (*A Midsummer Night's Dream 4.1*)

something ADV something here means somewhat or rather ❏ *Be something scanter of your maiden presence* (*Hamlet 1.3*)

sooth NOUN truly ❏ *Yes, sooth; and so do you* (*A Midsummer Night's Dream 3.2*)

spleen NOUN spleen means fury or anger ❏ *That, in a spleen, unfolds both heaven and earth* (*A Midsummer Night's Dream 1.1*)

sport NOUN sport means recreation or entertainment ❏ *I see our wars/ Will turn unto a peaceful comic sport* (*Henry VI part I 2.2*)

strain NOUN a strain is a tune or a musical phrase ❏ *and so die/ That strain again! it had a dying fall* (*Twelfth Night 1.1*)

suffer VERB in this context suffer means perish or die ❏ *but an islander that hath lately suffered by a thunderbolt.* (*The Tempest 2.2*)

suit NOUN a suit is a petition, request or proposal (marriage) ❏ *Because she will admit no kind of suit* (*Twelfth Night 1.2*)

sup VERB to sup is to have supper ❏ *Go know of Cassio where he supped tonight* (*Othello 5.1*)

surfeit NOUN a surfeit is an amount which is too large ❏ *If music be the food of love, play on;/ Give me excess of it, that, surfeiting,/ The appetite may sicken* (*Twelfth Night 1.1*)

swain NOUN a swain is a suitor or person who wants to marry ❏ *take this transformed scalp/ From off the head of this Athenian swain* (*A Midsummer Night's Dream 4.1*)

thereto ADV thereto meant also ❏ *If she be black, and thereto have a wit* (*Othello 2.1*)

throstle NOUN a throstle was a name for a song-bird ❏ *The throstle with his note so true* (*A Midsummer Night's Dream 3.1*)

tidings NOUN tidings meant news ❏ *that upon certain tidings now arrived, importing the mere perdition of the Turkish fleet* (*Othello 2.2*)

transgress VERB if you transgress you break a moral law or rule of behaviour ❏ *Virtue that transgresses is but patched with sin* (*Twelfth Night 1.5*)

troth, by my PHRASE this phrase means I swear or in truth or on my word ❏ *By my troth, Sir Toby, you must come in earlier o' nights* (*Twelfth Night 1.3*)

trumpery NOUN trumpery means things that look expensive but are worth nothing (often clothing) ❏ *The trumpery in my house, go bring it hither/ For stale catch these thieves* (*The Tempest 4.1*)

twink NOUN In the wink of an eye or no time at all ❏ *Ay, with a twink* (*The Tempest 4.1*)

undone ADJ if something or someone is undone they are ruined, destroyed, brought down ❏ *You have undone a man of fourscore three* (*The Winter's Tale 4.4*)

varlets NOUN varlets were villains or ruffians ❏ *Say again: where didst thou leave these varlets?* (*The Tempest 4.1*)

vaward NOUN the vaward is an old word for the vanguard, front part or earliest ❏ *And since we have the vaward of the day* (*A Midsummer Night's Dream 4.1*)

visage NOUN face ❏ *when Phoebe doth behold/Her silver visage in the watery glass* (*A Midsummer Night's Dream 1.1*)

voice NOUN voice means vote ❏ *He has our voices* (*Coriolanus 2.3*)

waggish ADJ waggish means playful ❏ *As waggish boys in game themselves forswear* (*A Midsummer Night's Dream 1.1*)

wane VERB to wane is to vanish, go down or get slighter. It is most often used to describe a phase of the moon ❏ *but, O, methinks, how slow/This old moon wanes* (*A Midsummer Night's Dream 1.1*)

want VERB to want means to lack or to be without ❏ *a beast that wants discourse of reason/Would have mourned longer* (*Hamlet 1.2*)

warrant VERB to assure, promise, guarantee ❏ *I warrant your grace* (*As You Like It 1.2*)

welkin NOUN welkin is an old word for the sky or the heavens ❏ *The starry welkin cover thou anon/With drooping fog as black as Acheron* (*A Midsummer Night's Dream 3.2*)

wench NOUN wench is an old word for a girl ❏ *Well demanded, wench* (*The Tempest 1.2*)

whence ADV from where ❏ *Whence came you, sir?* (*Twelfth Night 1.5*)

wherefore ADV why ❏ *Wherefore, sweetheart? what's your metaphor?* (*Twelfth Night 1.3*)

wide-chopped ADJ if you were wide-chopped you were big-mouthed ❏ *This wide-chopped rascal* (*The Tempest 1.1*)

wight NOUN wight is an old word for person or human being ❏ *She was a wight, if ever such wight were* (*Othello 2.1*)

wit NOUN wit means intelligence or wisdom ❏ *thou didst conclude hairy men plain dealers, without wit* (*The Comedy of Errors 2.2*)

wits NOUN wits mean mental sharpness ❏ *we that have good wits have much to answer for* (*As You Like It 4.1*)

wont ADJ to wont is to be in the habit of doing something regularly ❏ *When were you wont to use my sister thus?* (*The Comedy of Errors 2.2*)

wooer NOUN a wooer is a suitor, someone who is hoping to marry ❏ *and of a foolish knight that you brought in one night here to be her wooer* (*Twelfth Night 1.3*)

wot VERB wot is an old word which means know or learn ❏ *for well I wot/Thou runnest before me* (*A Midsummer Night's Dream 3.2*)